THIS BOOK BELONGS TO

NAME :

AGE :

ADDRESS :

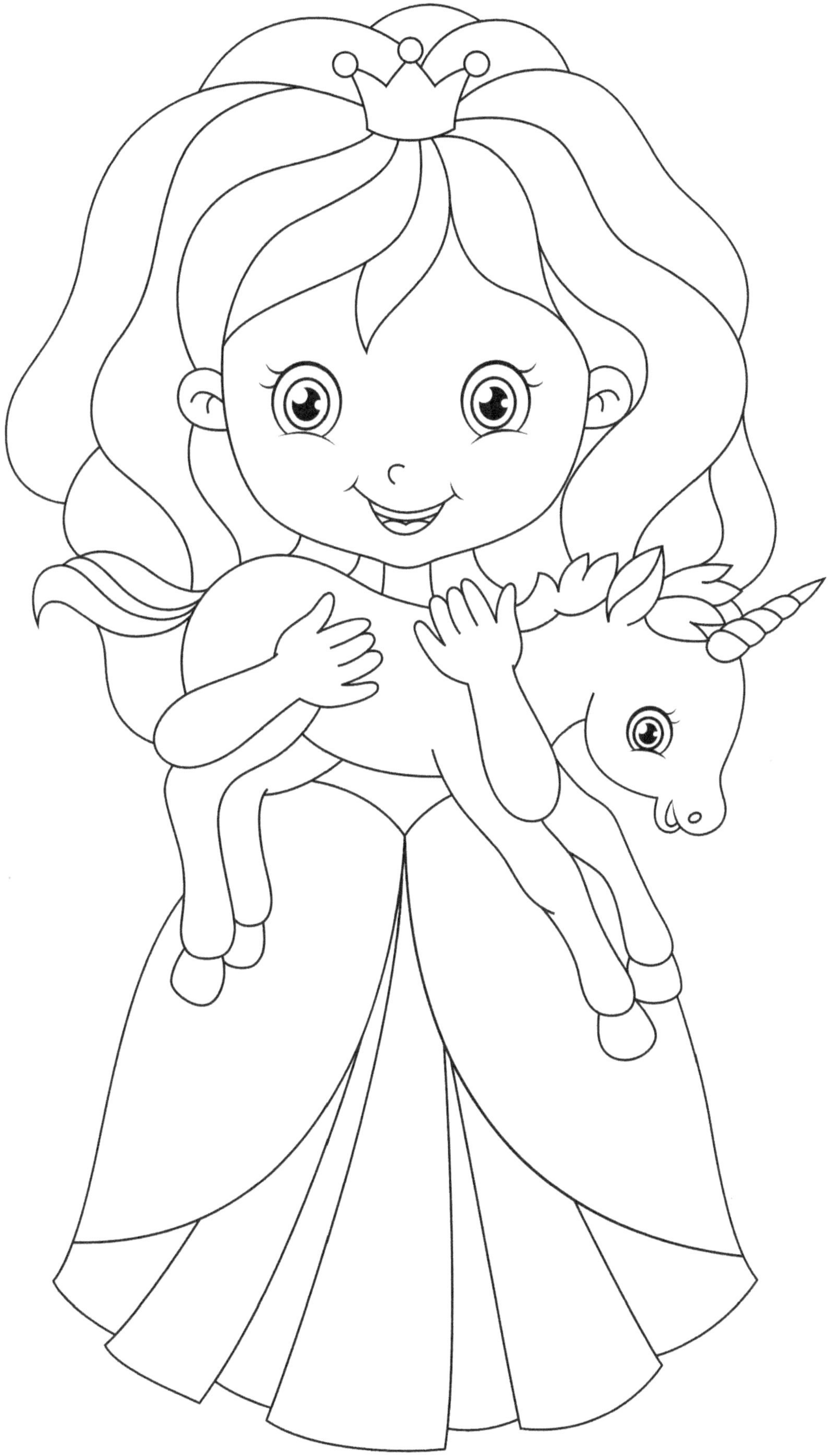

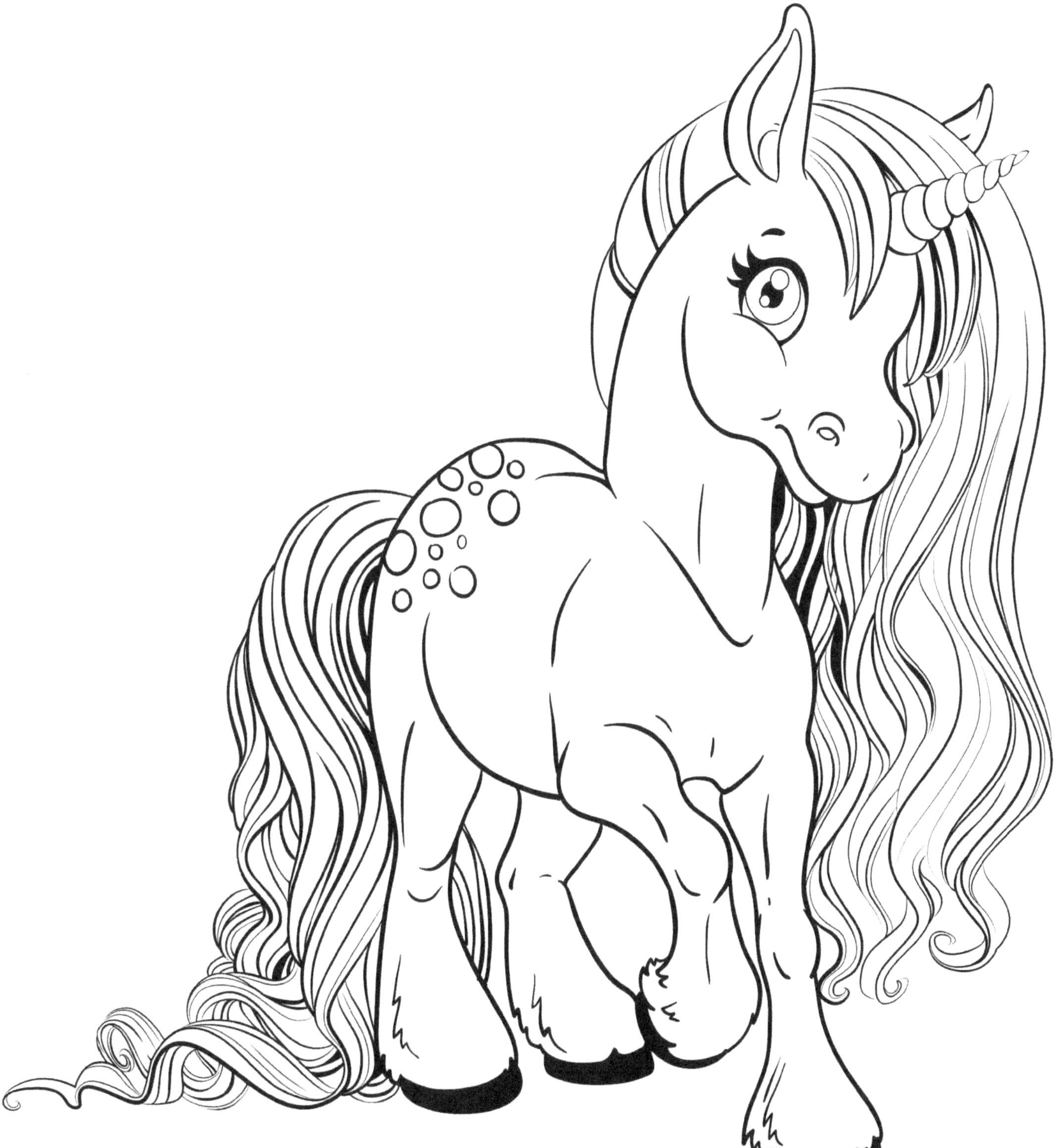

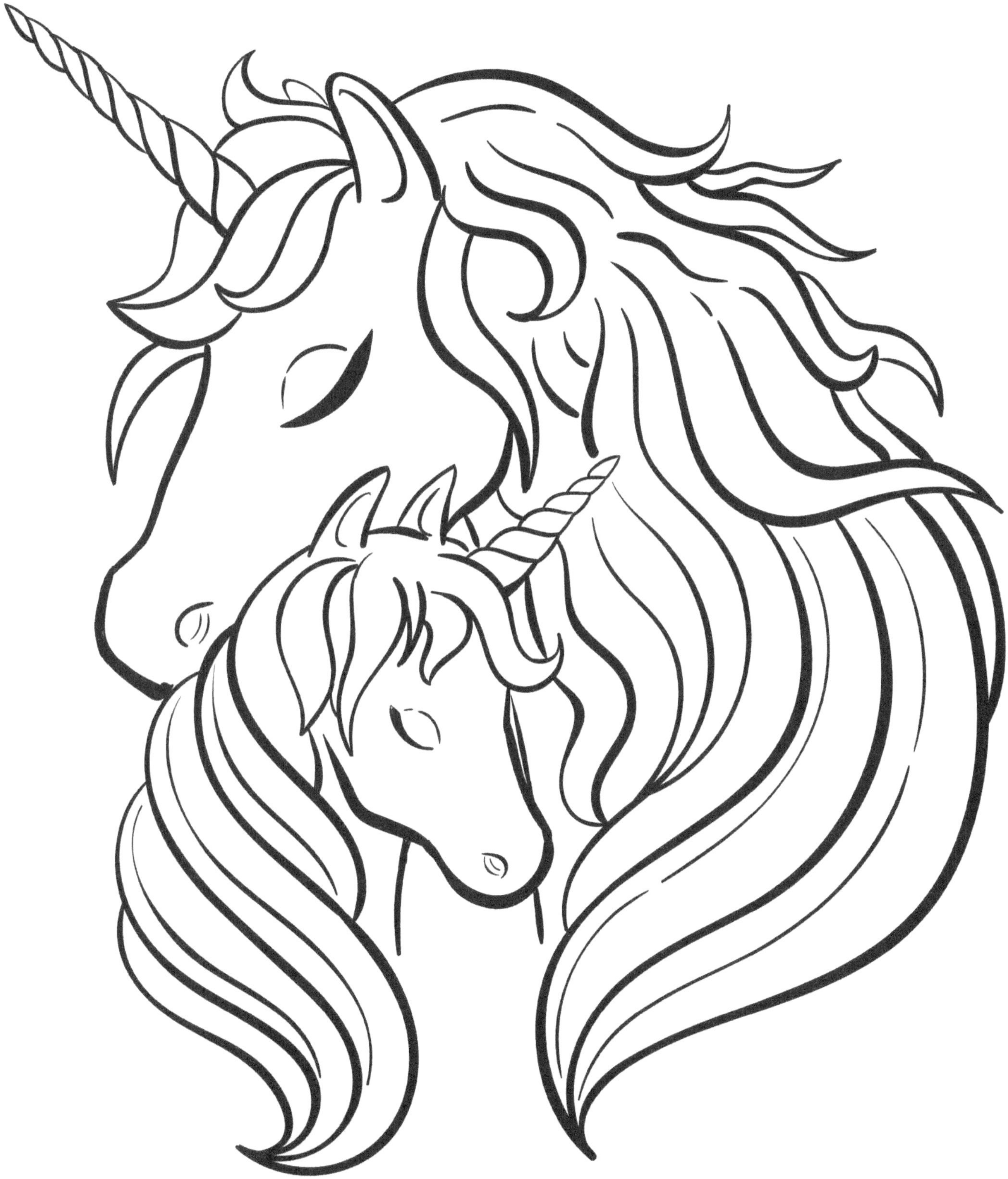

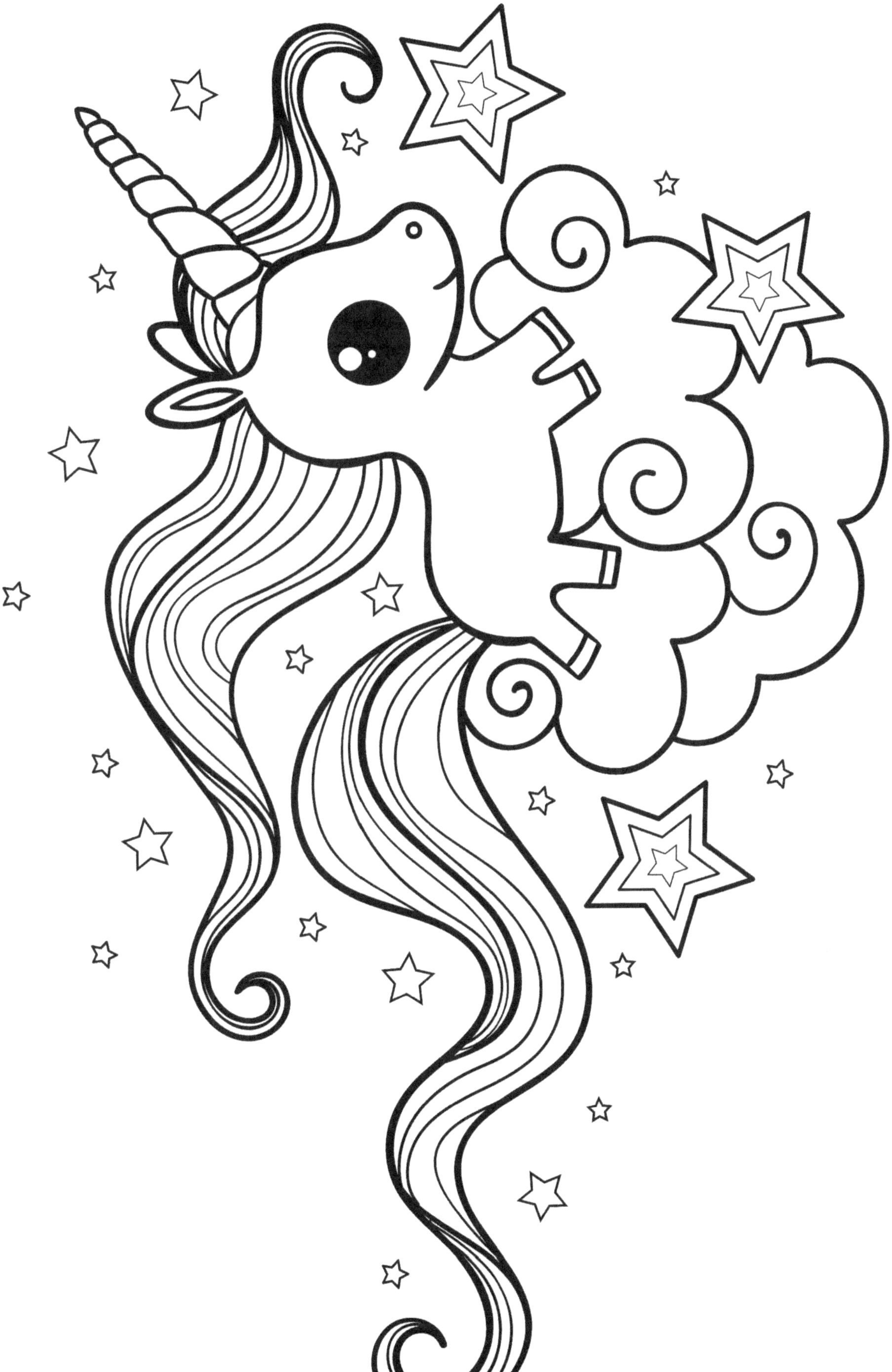

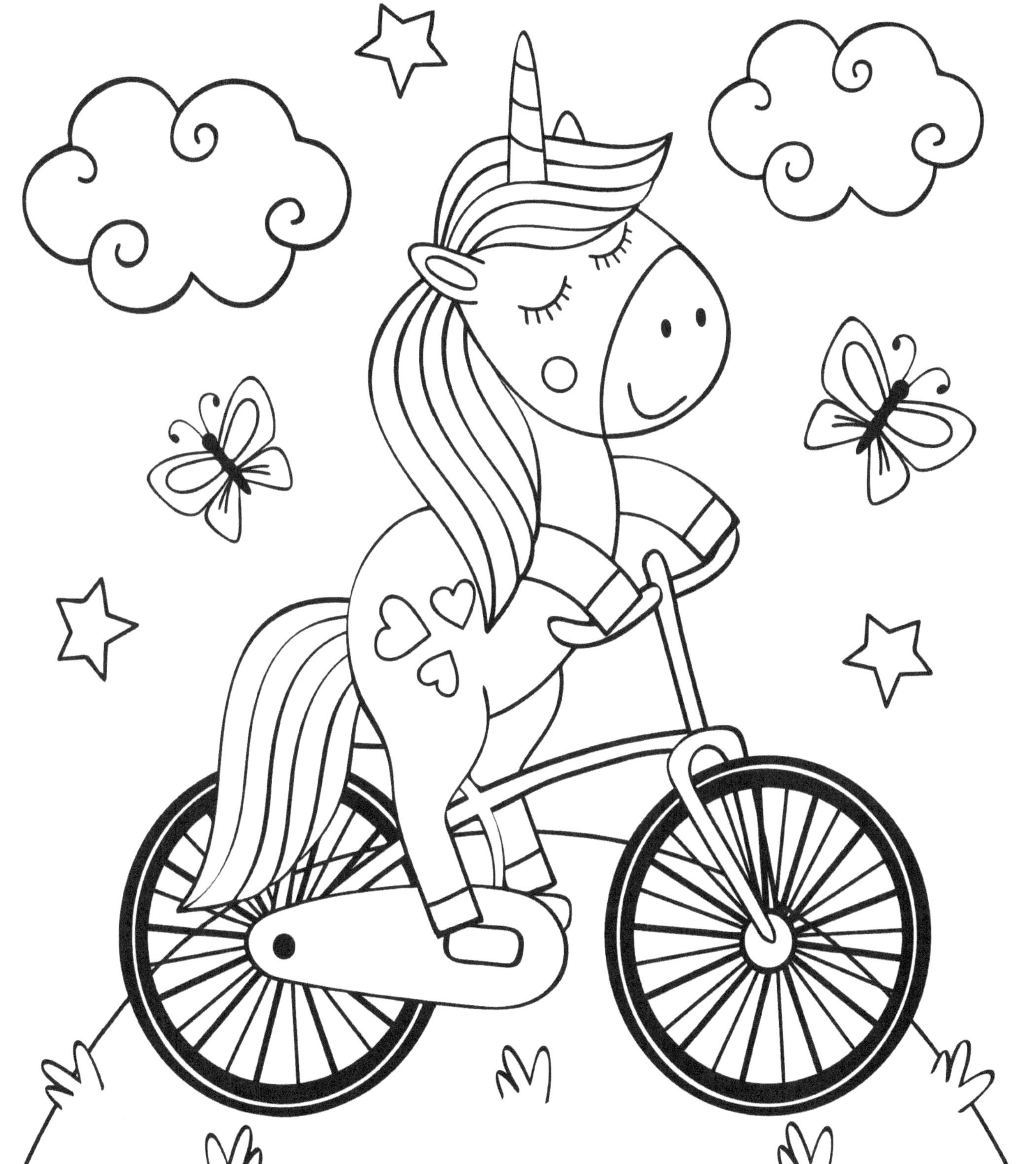

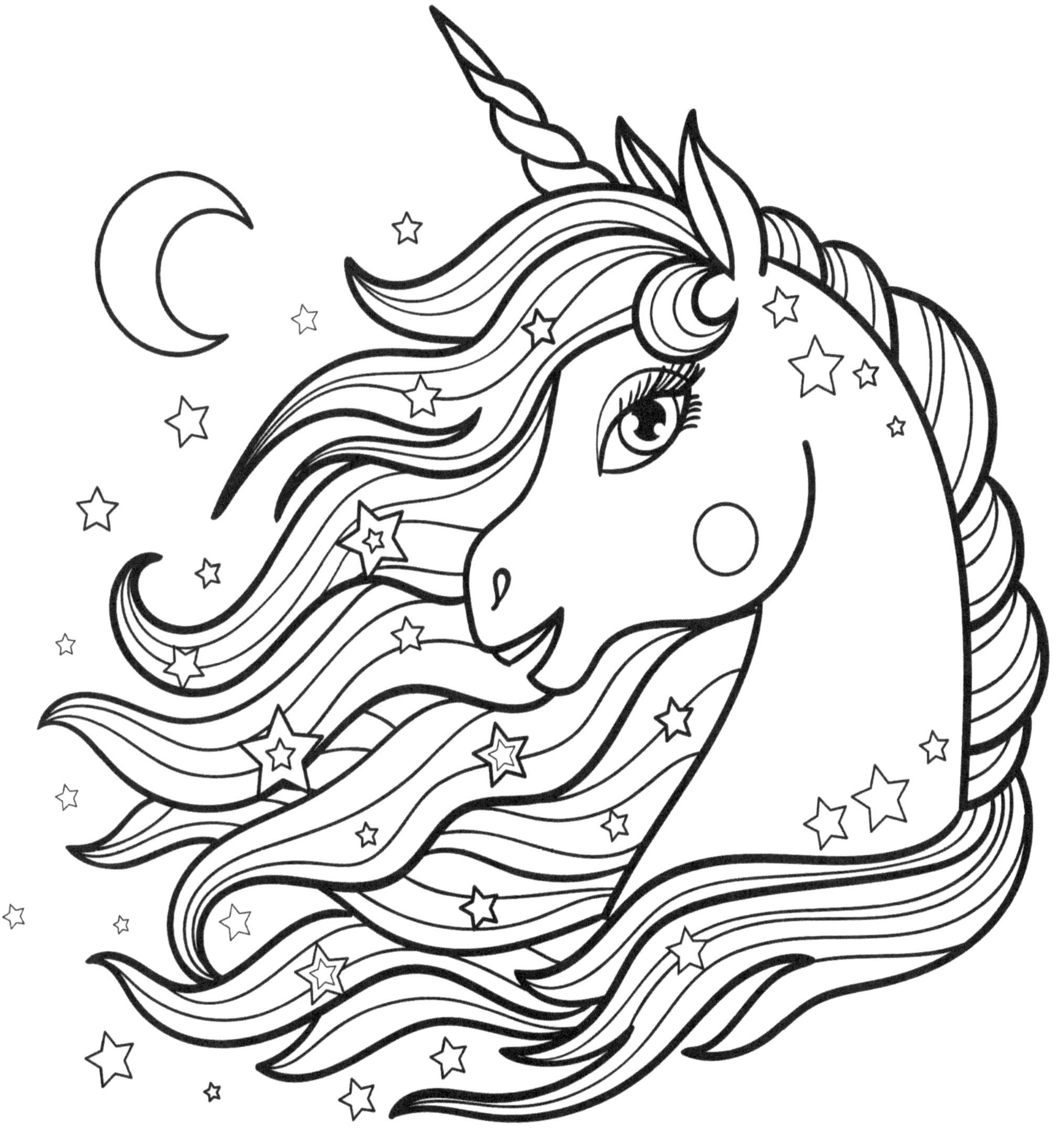

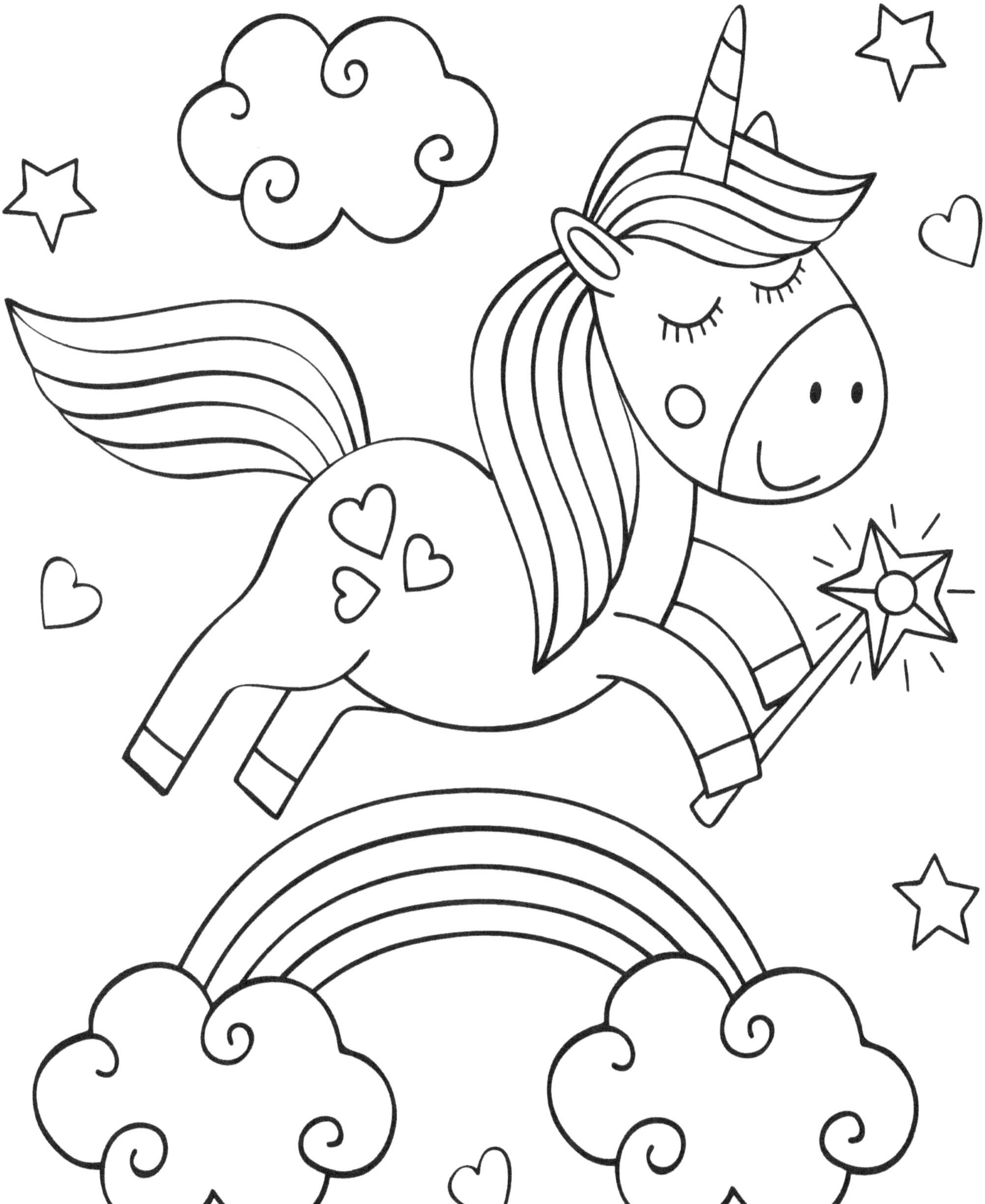

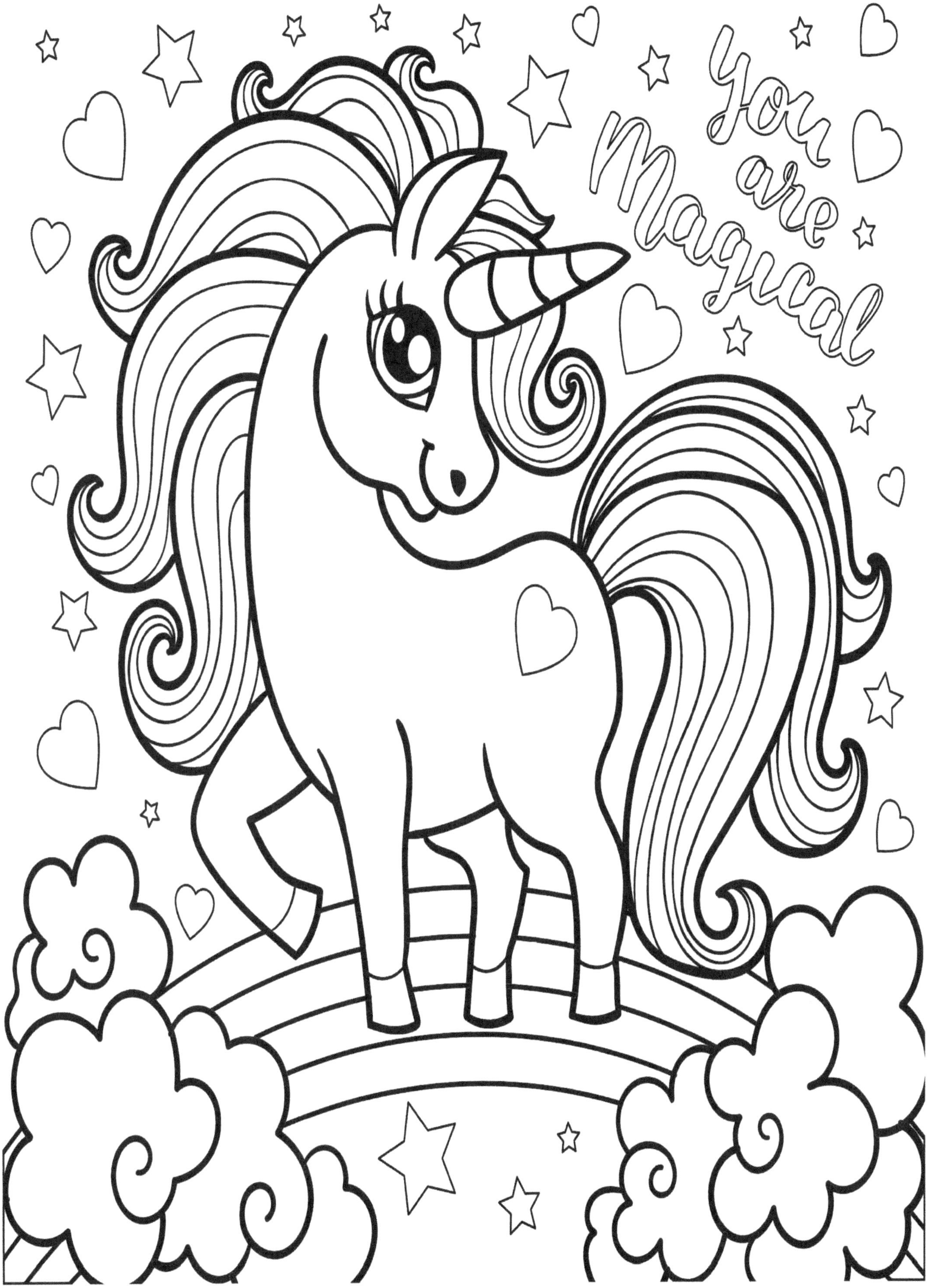
You are Magical

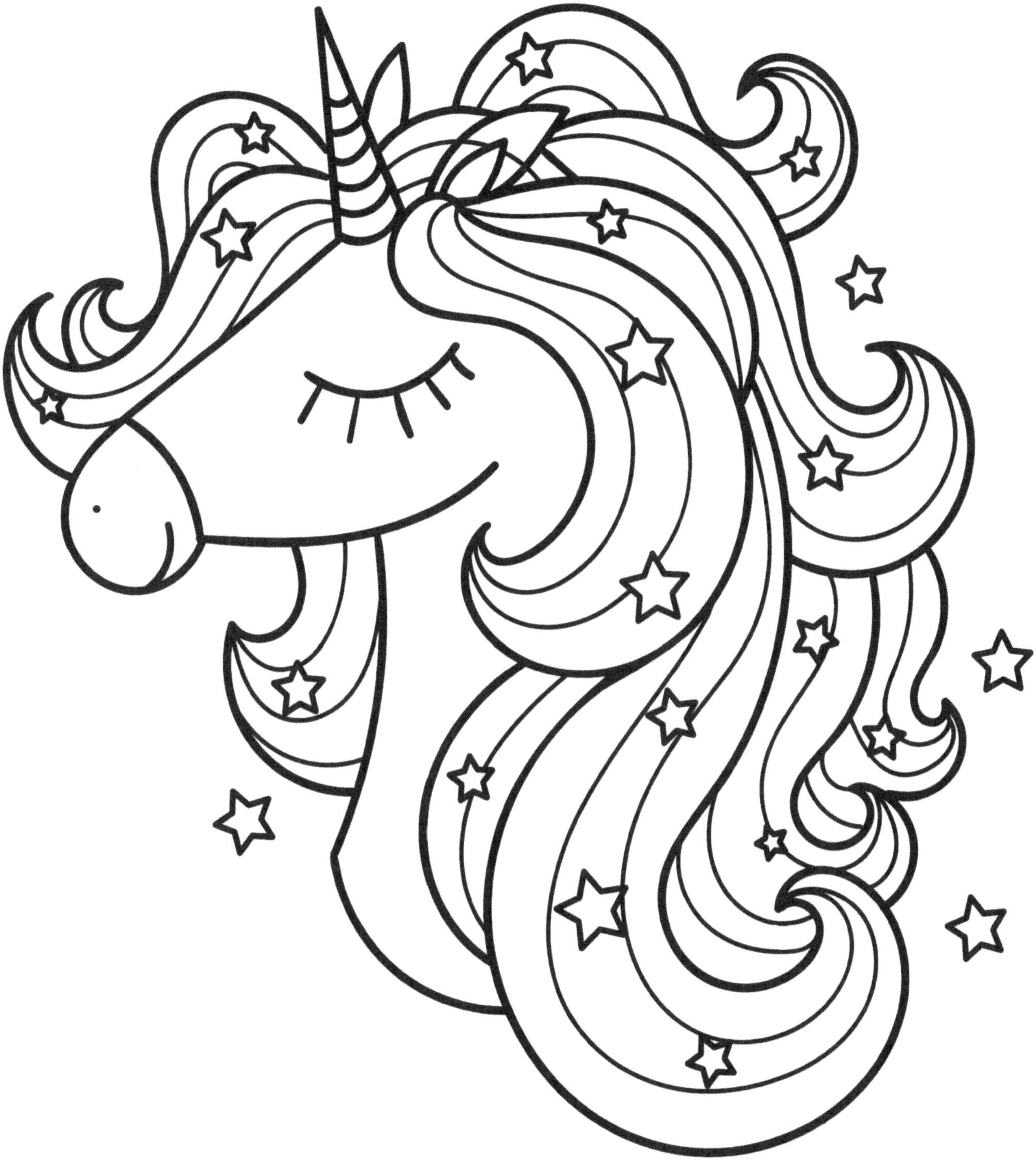

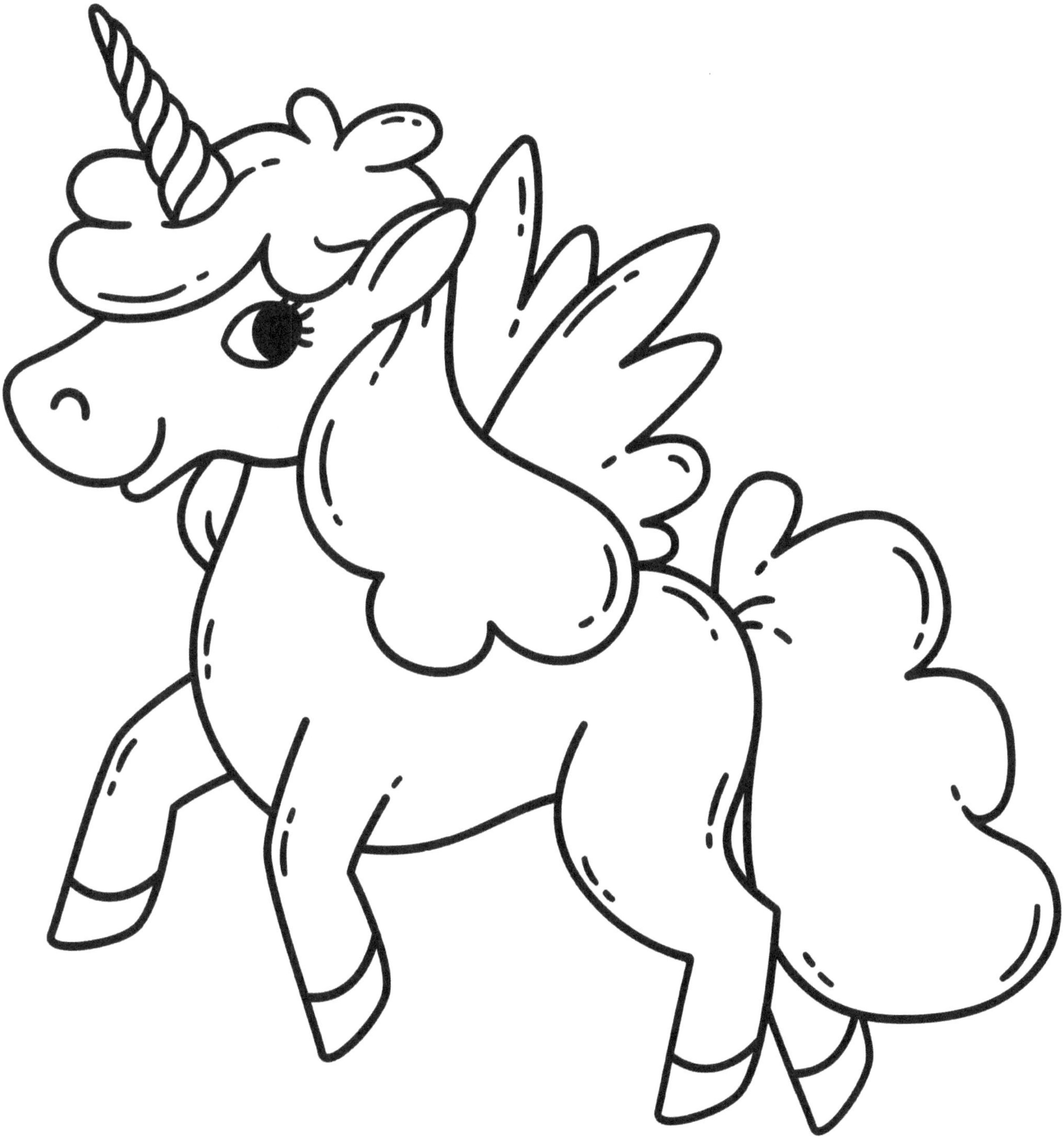

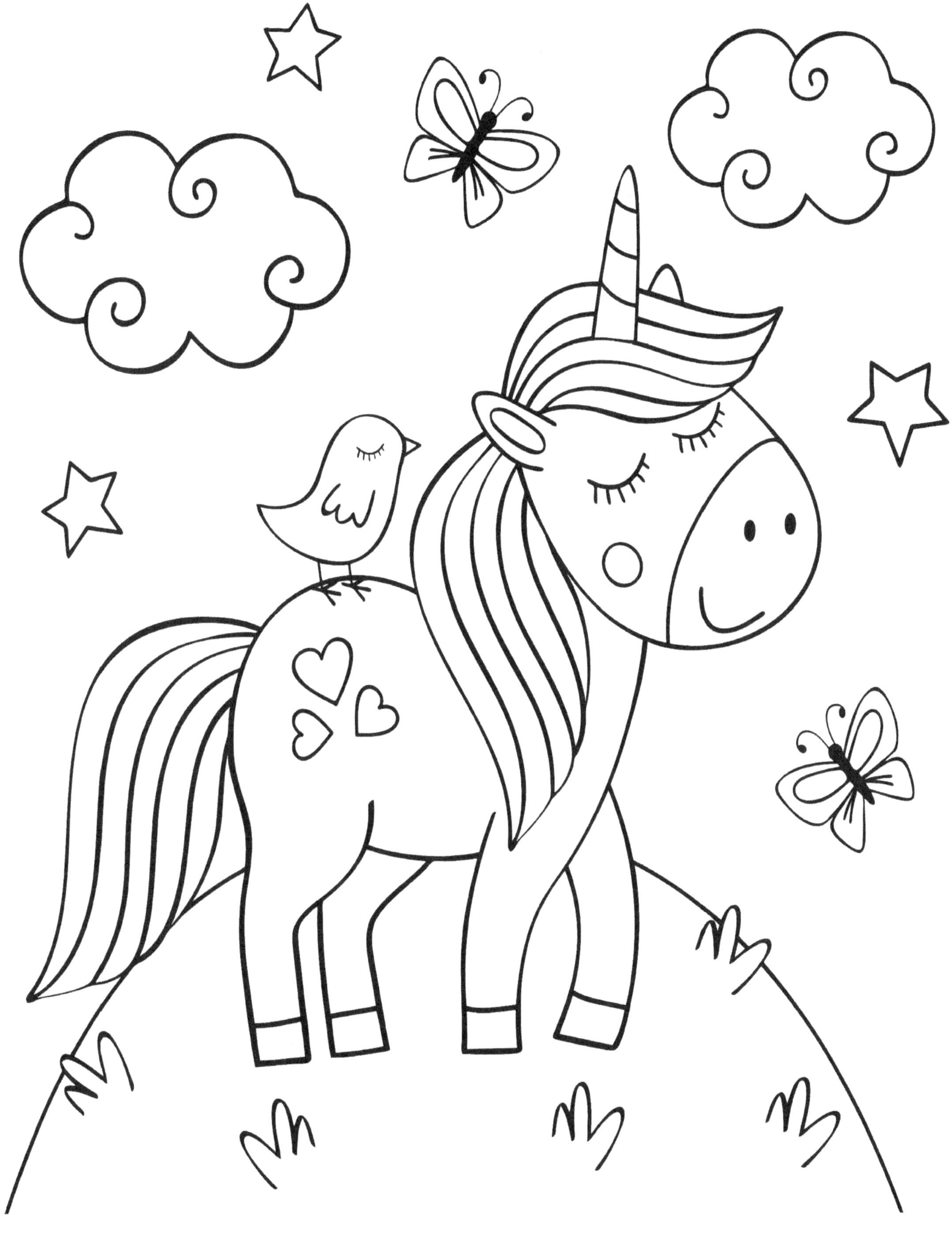

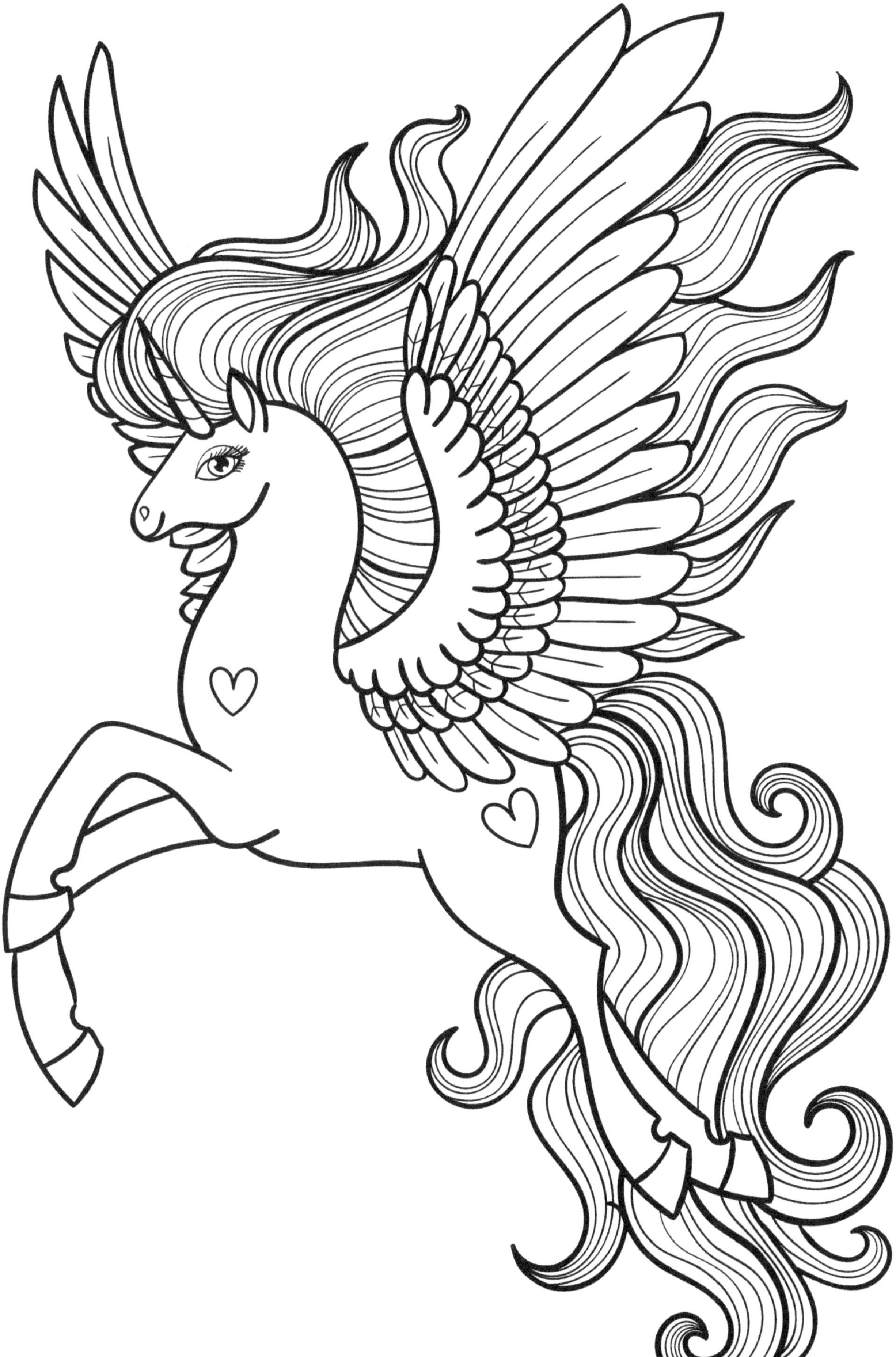

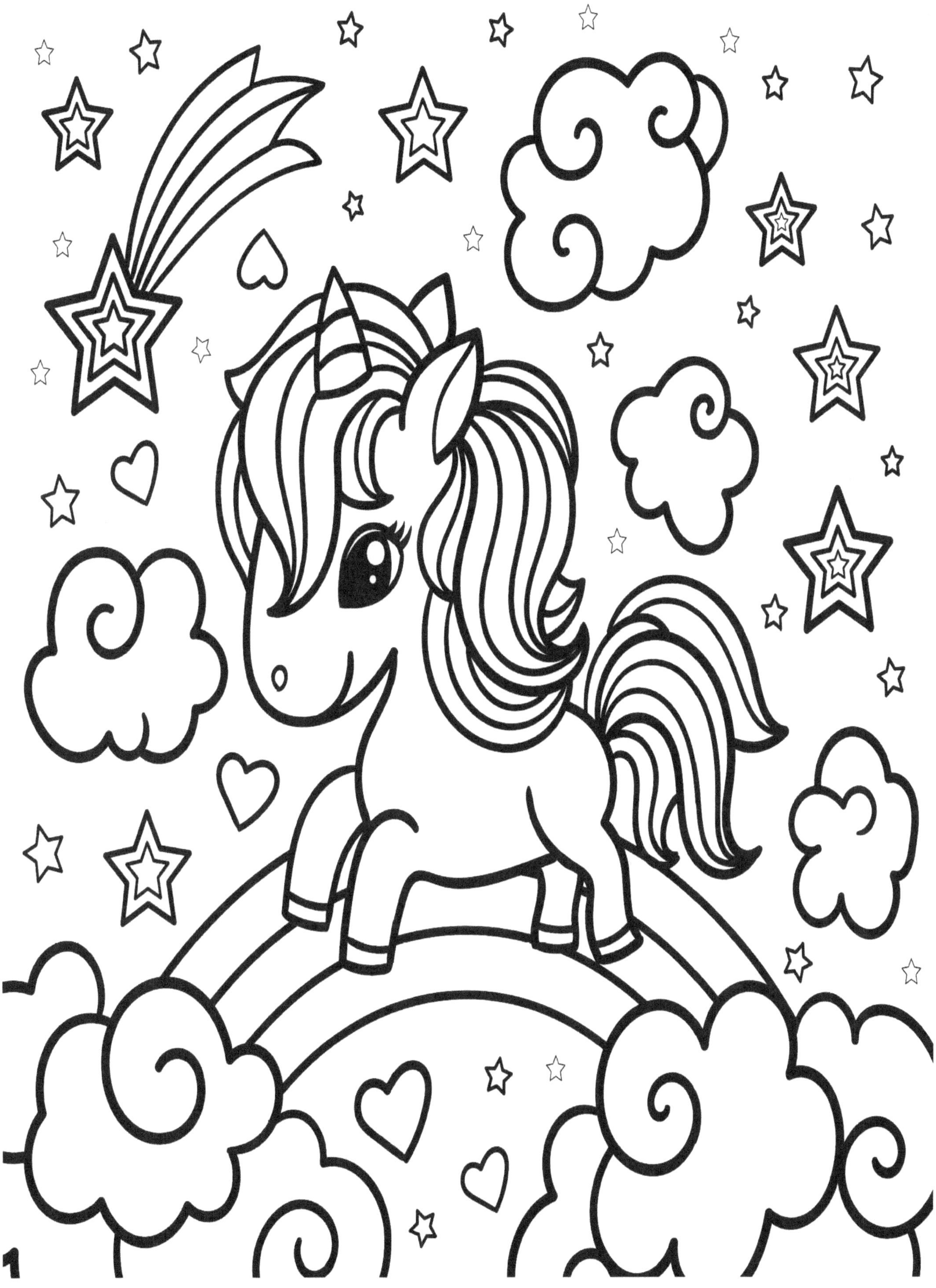

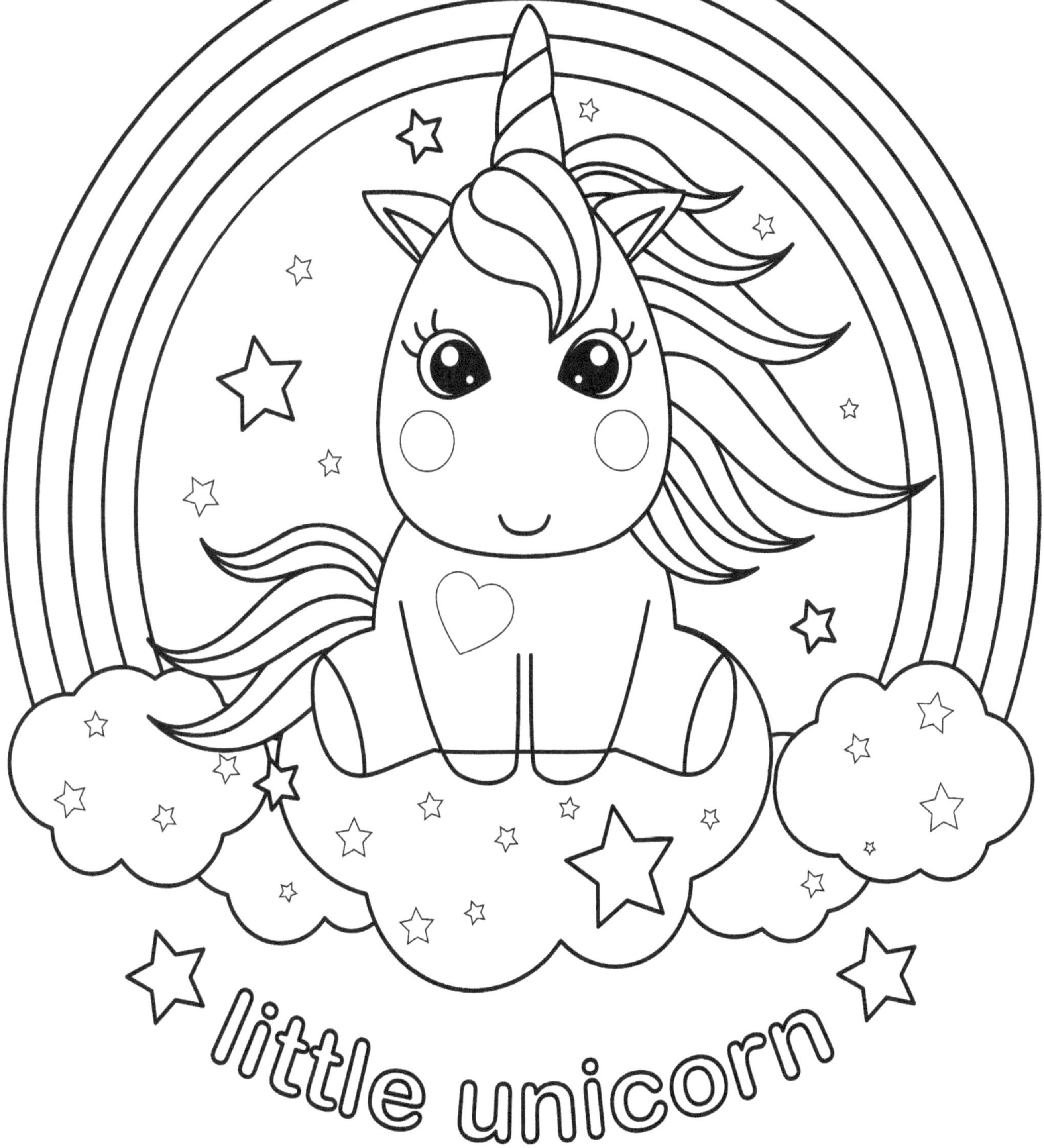
little unicorn

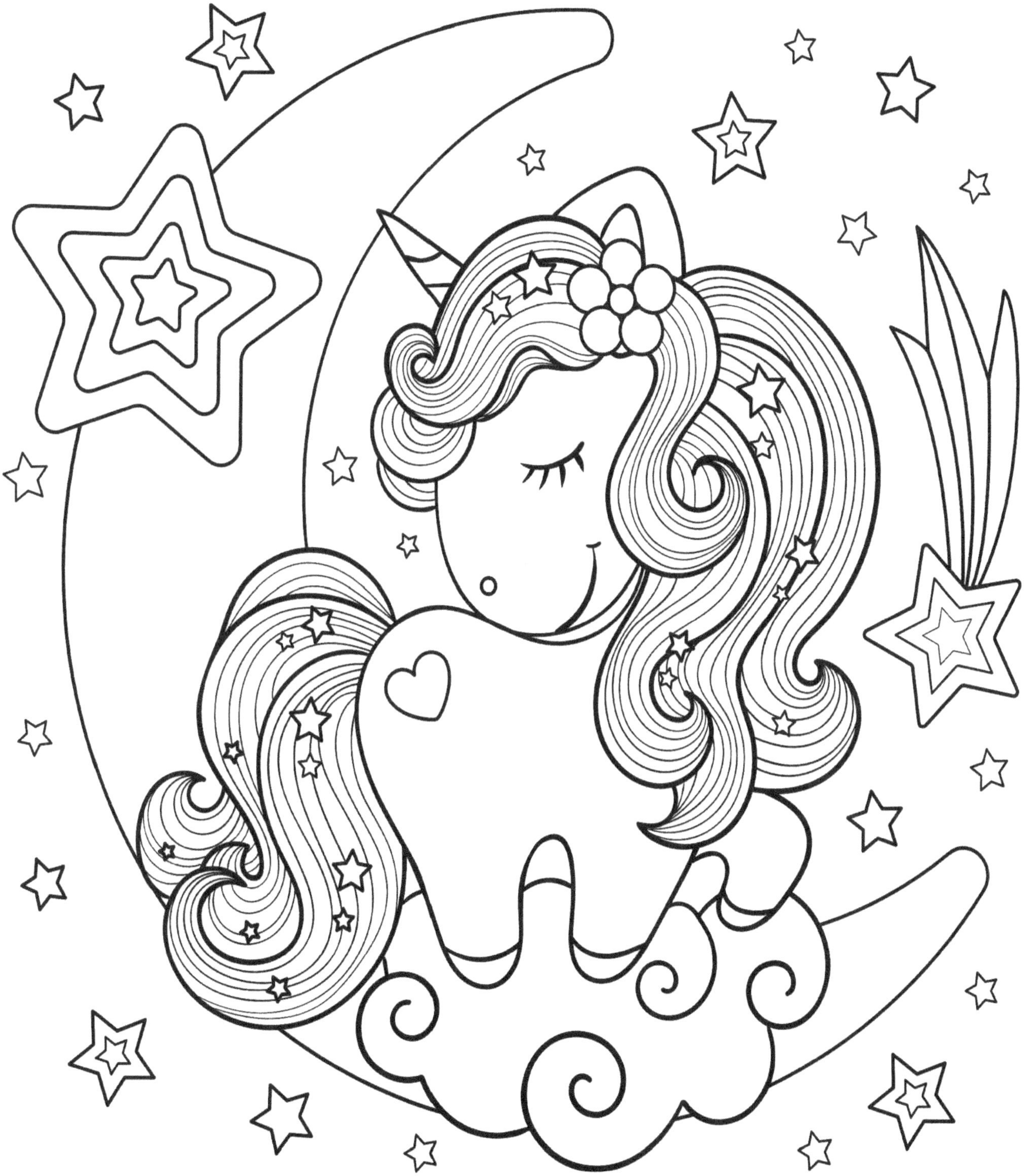

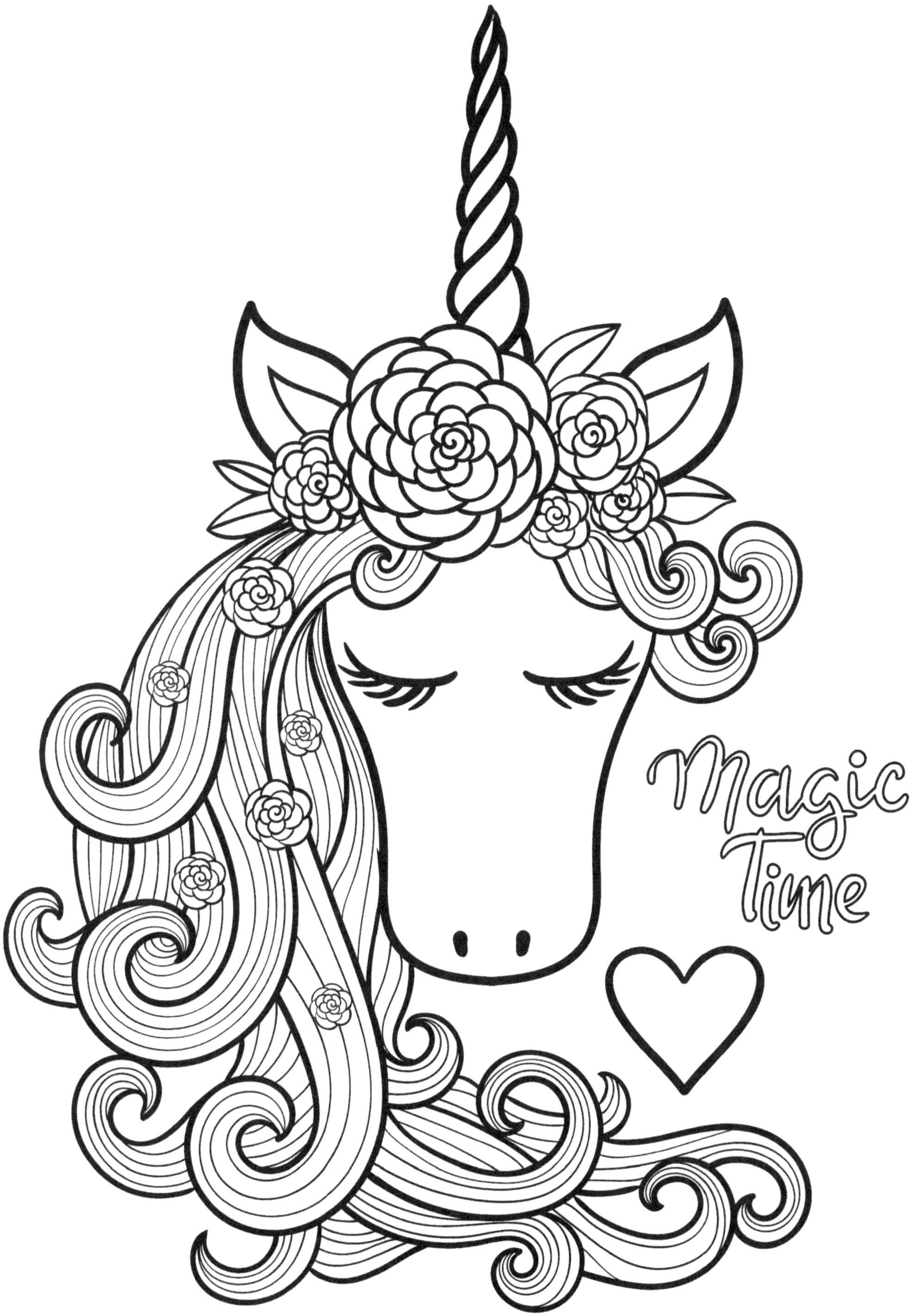
Magic
Time

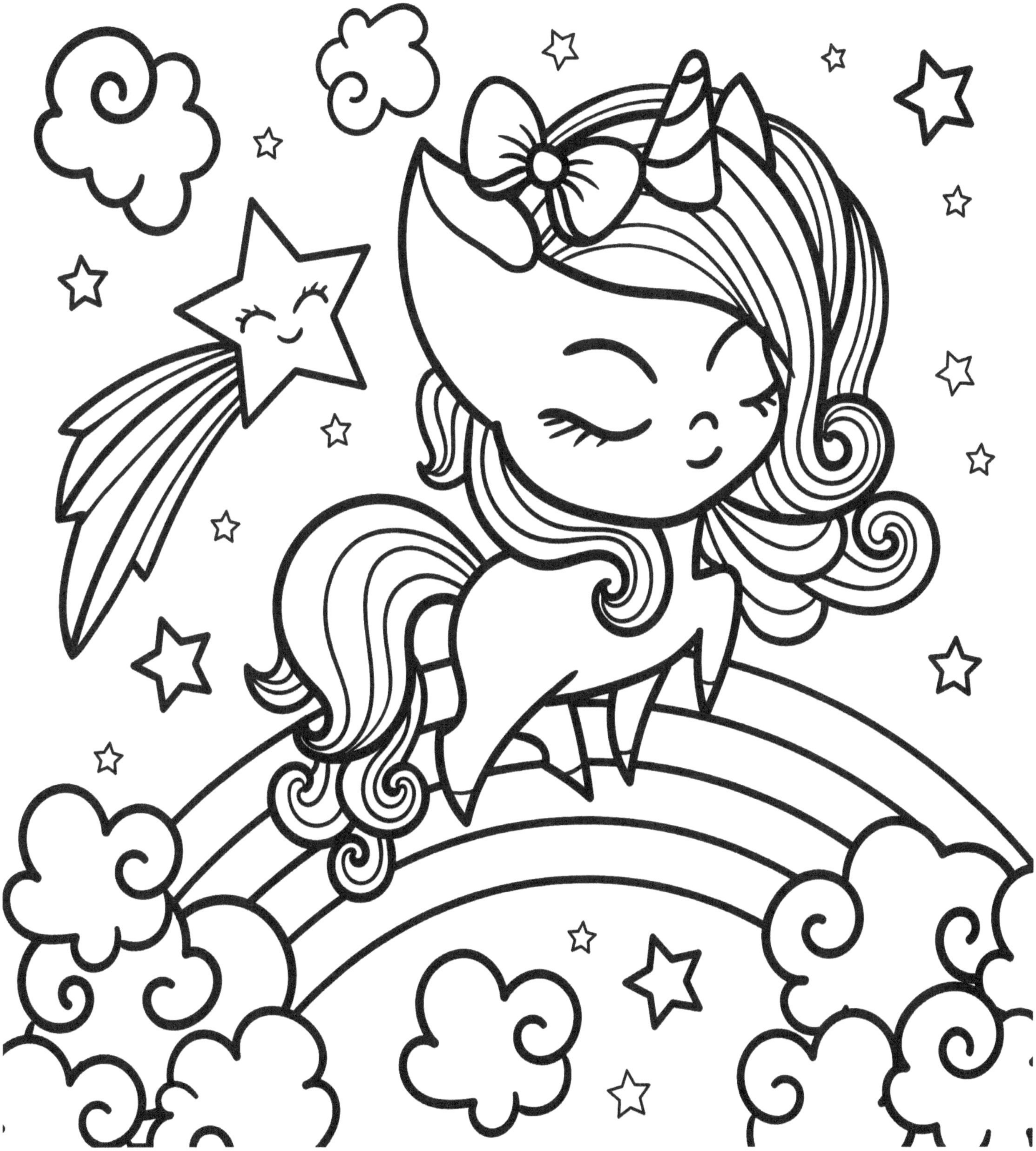

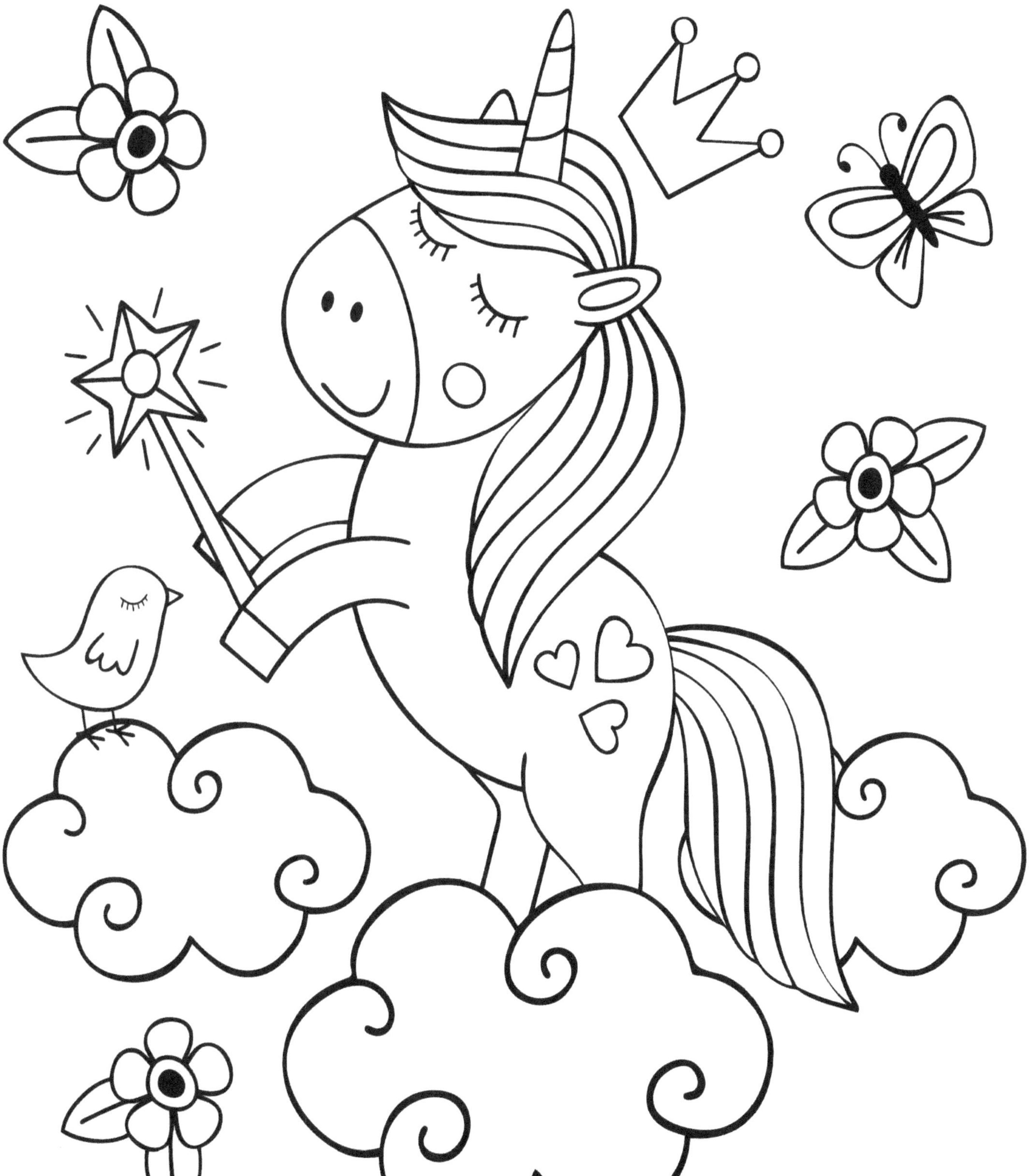

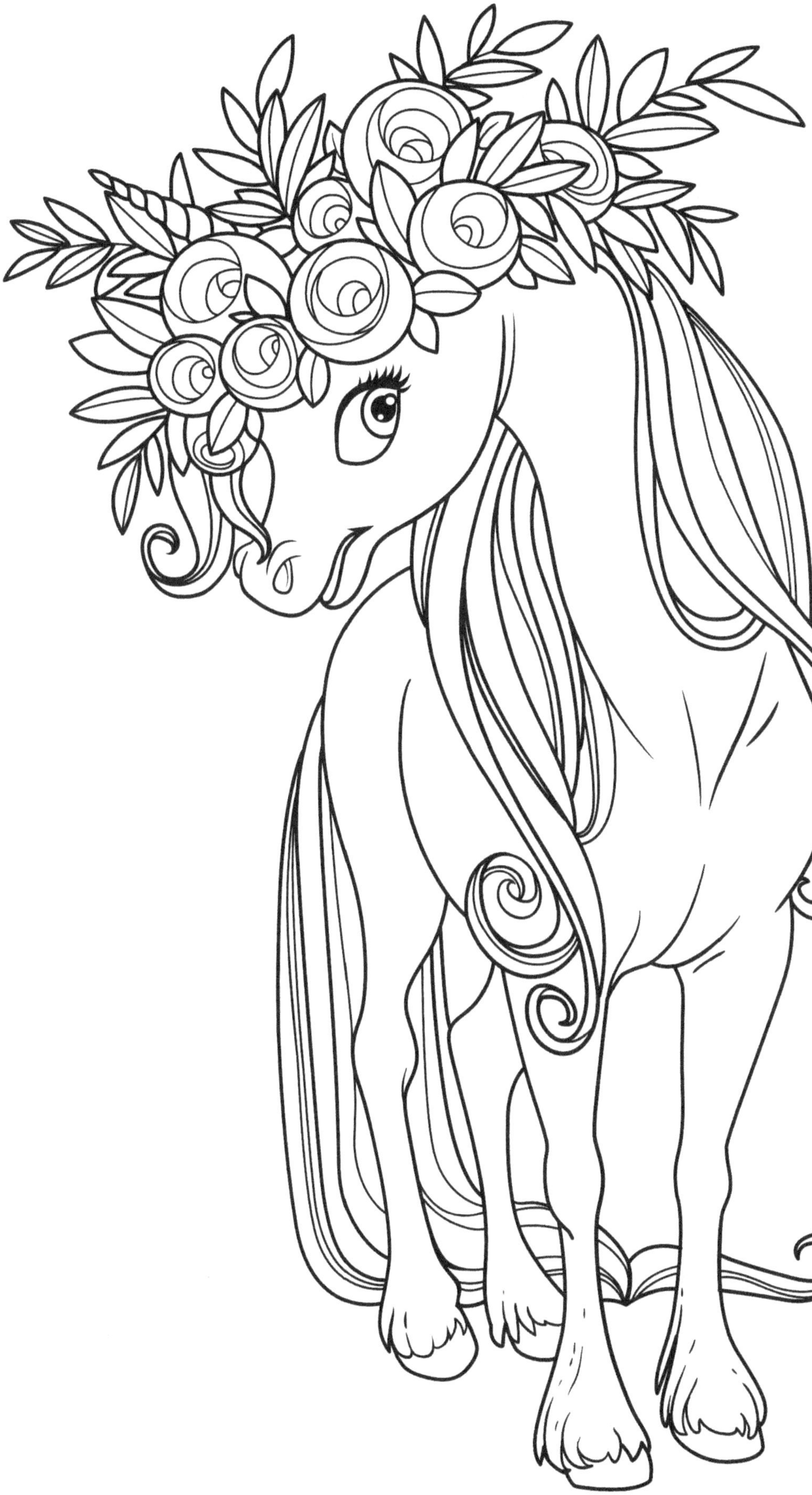

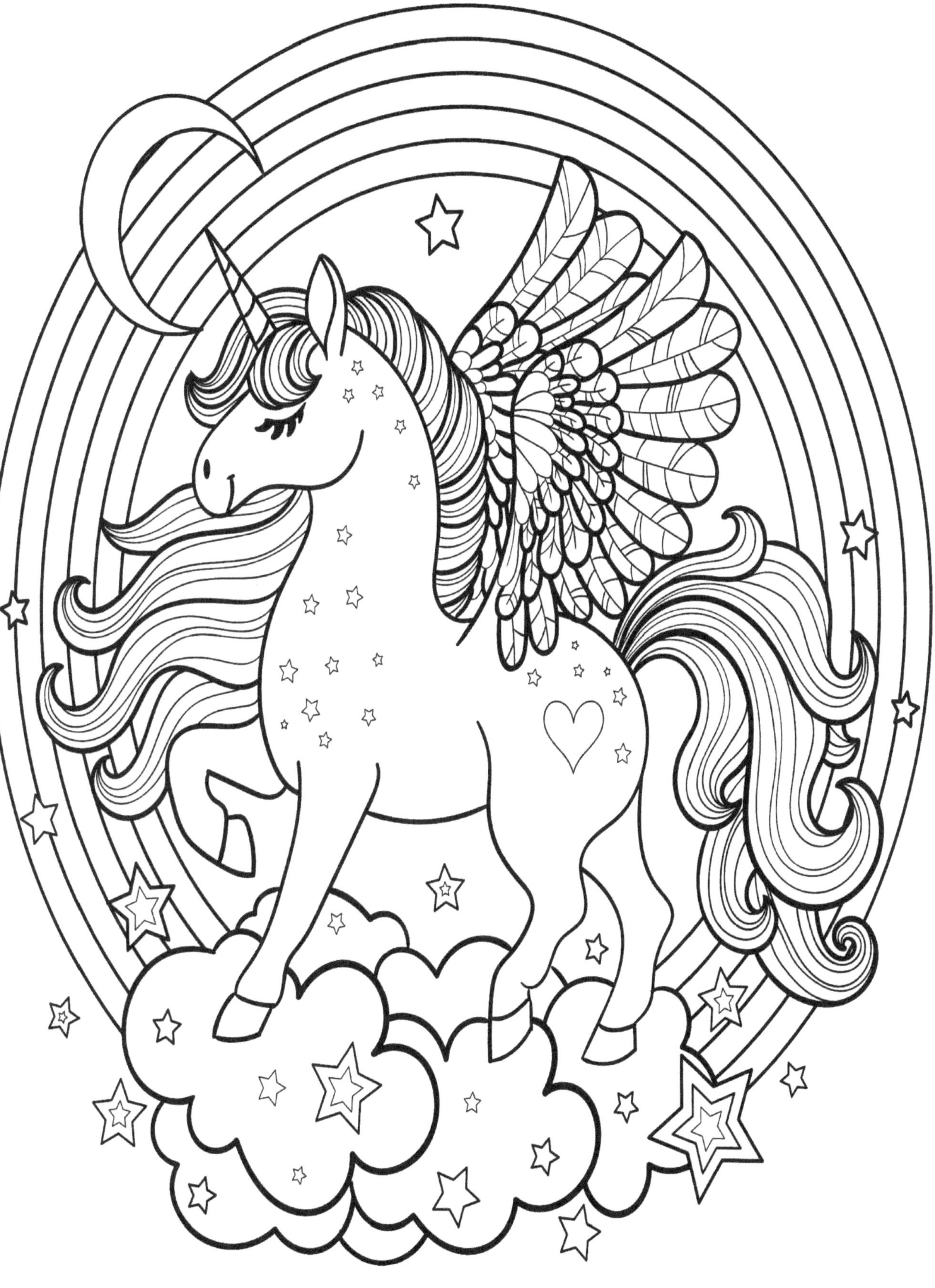

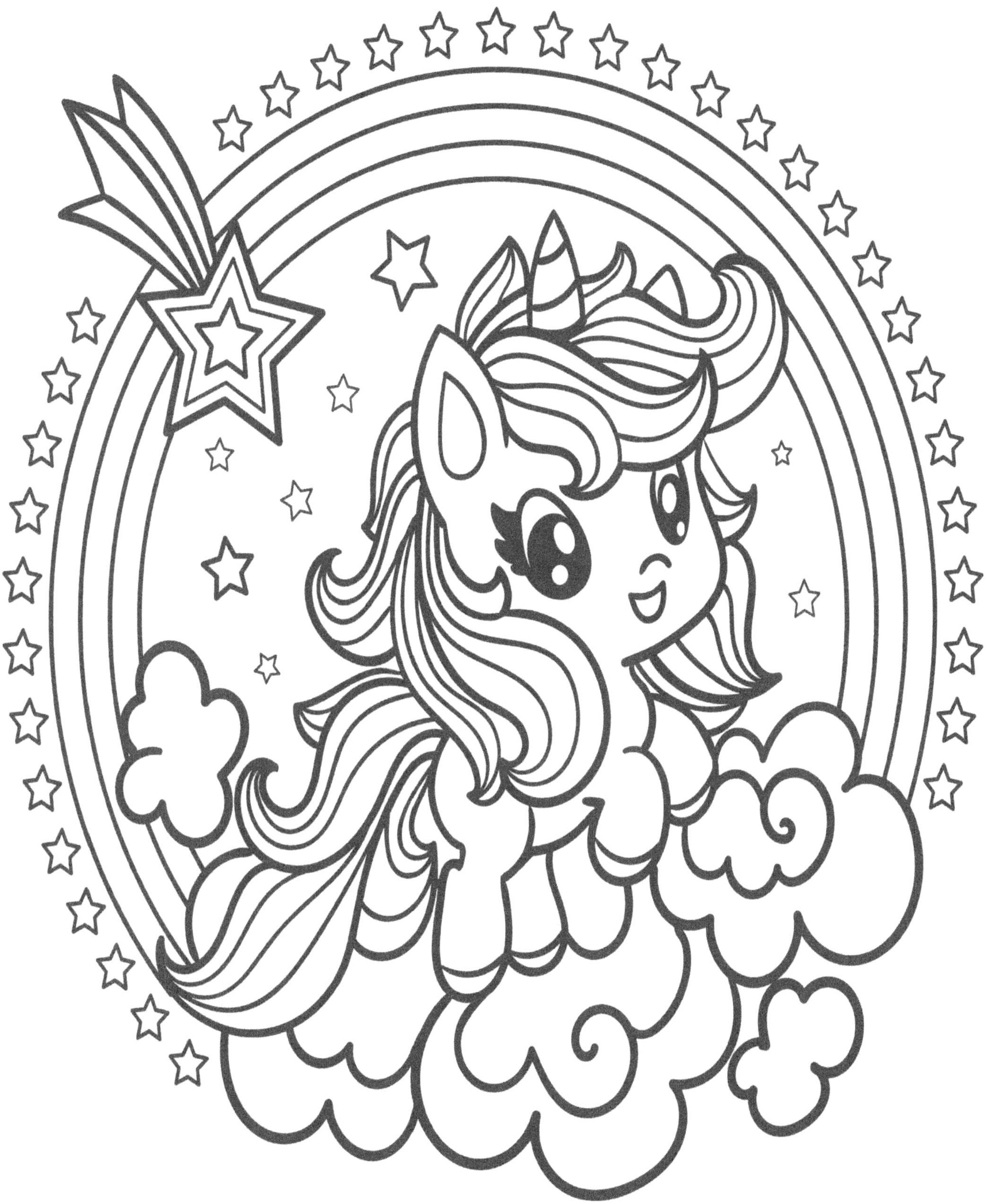

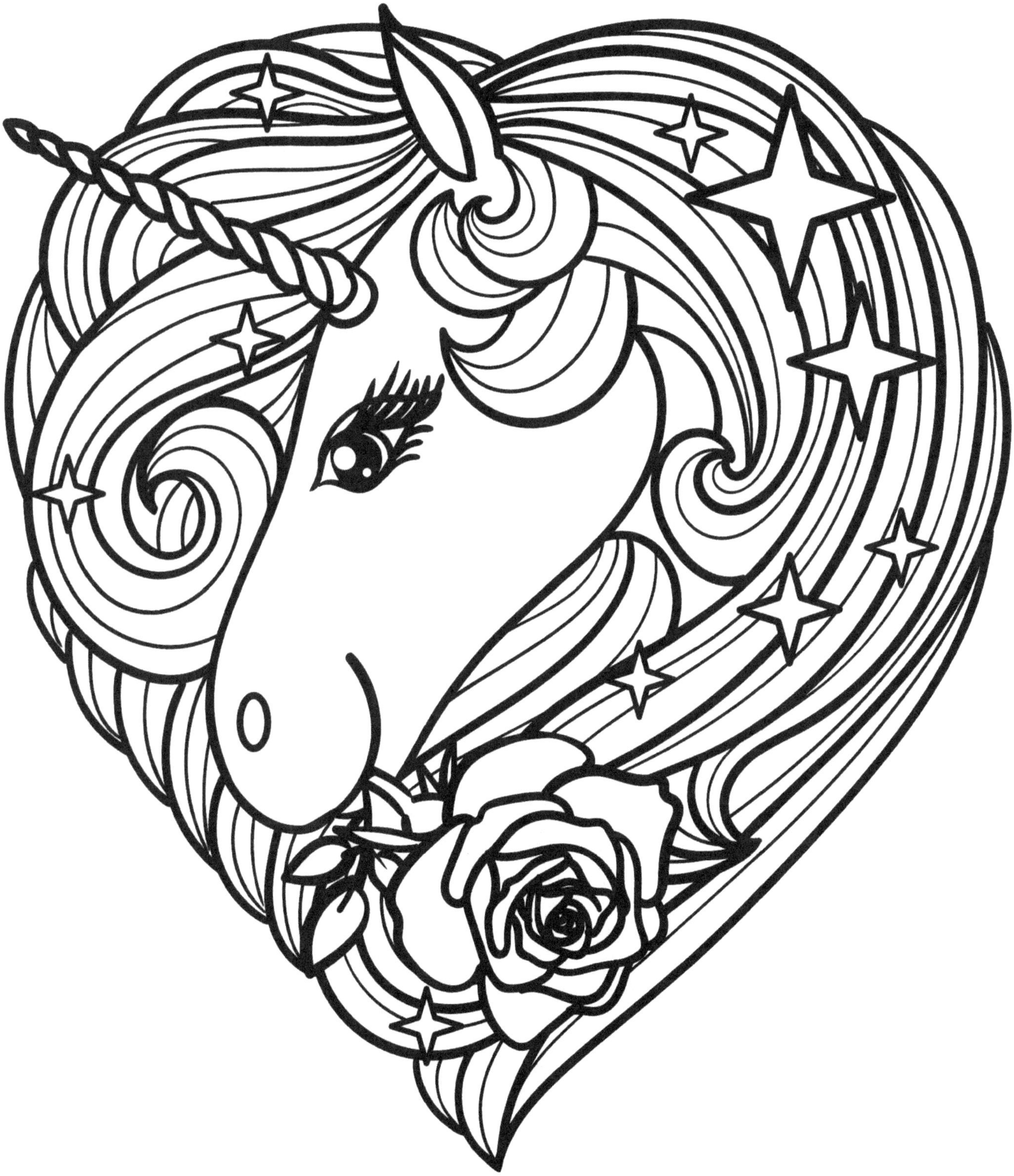

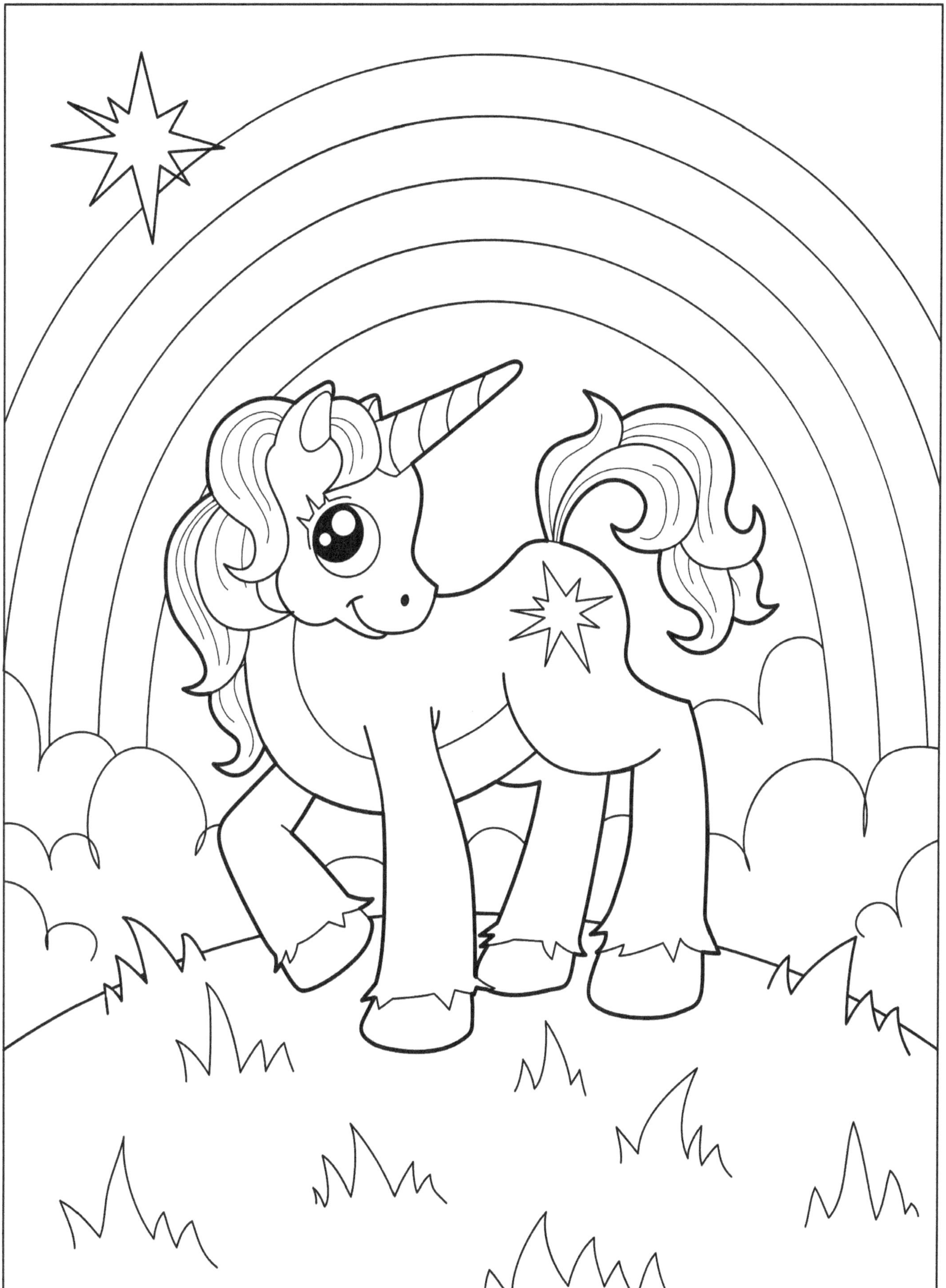

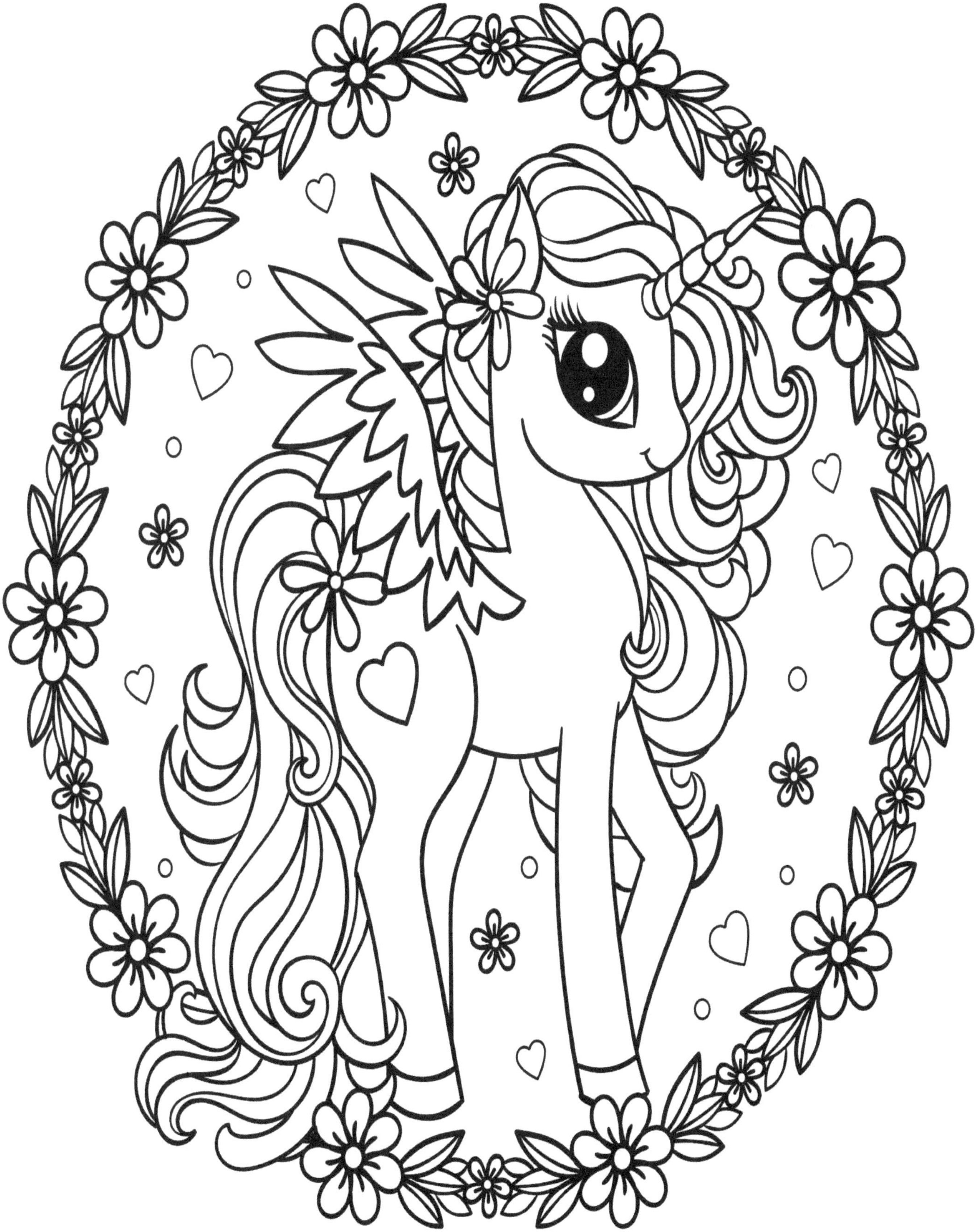

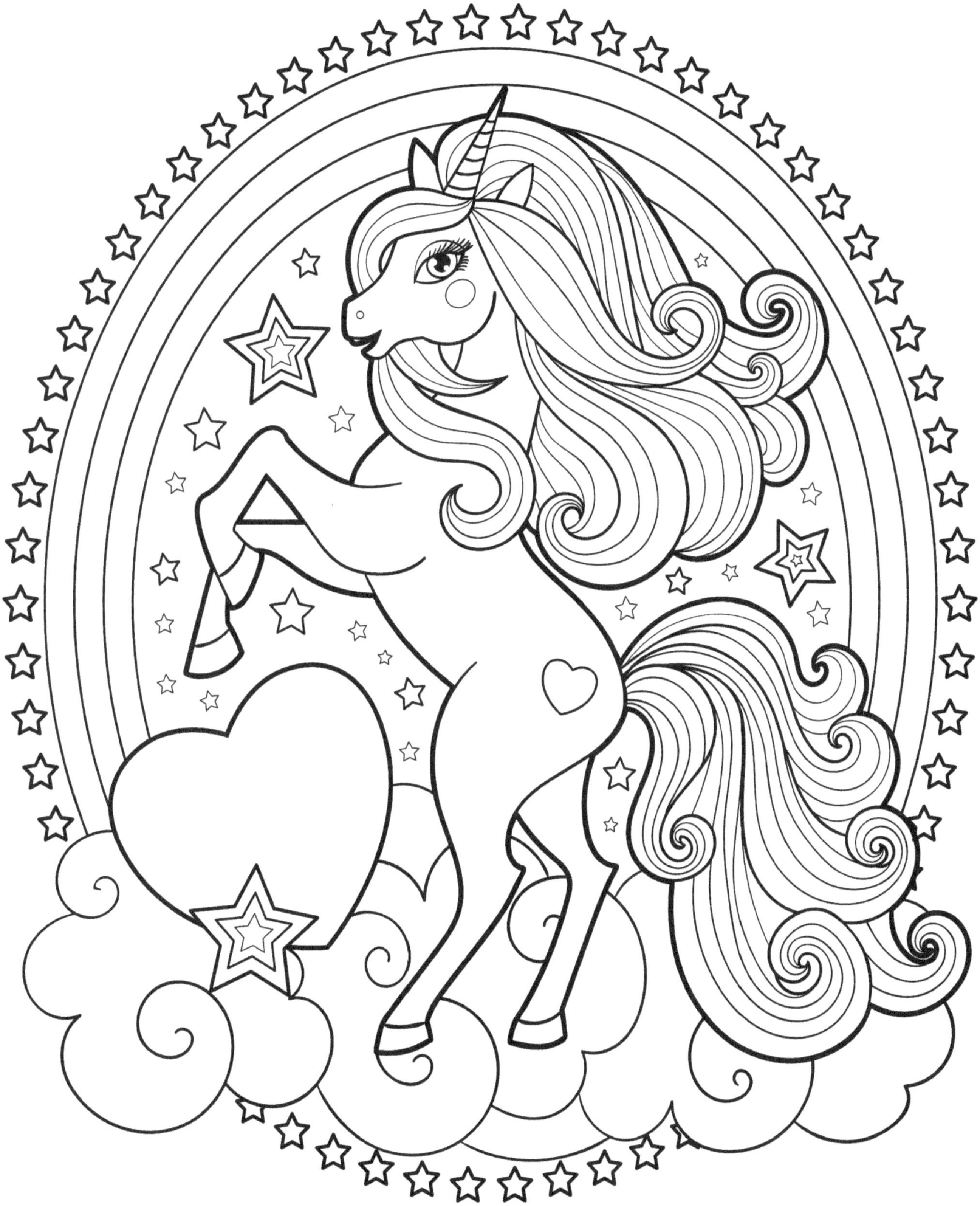

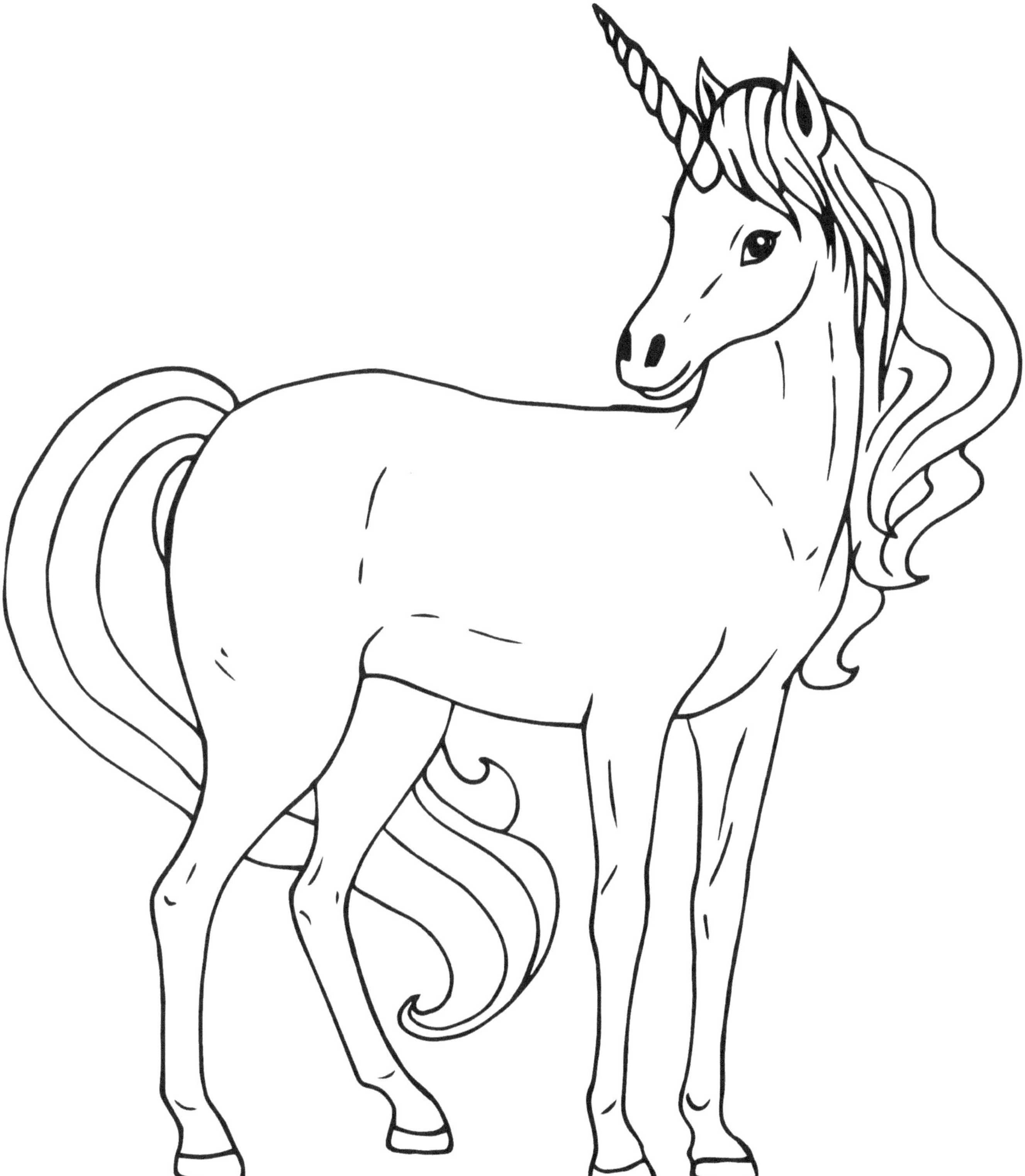

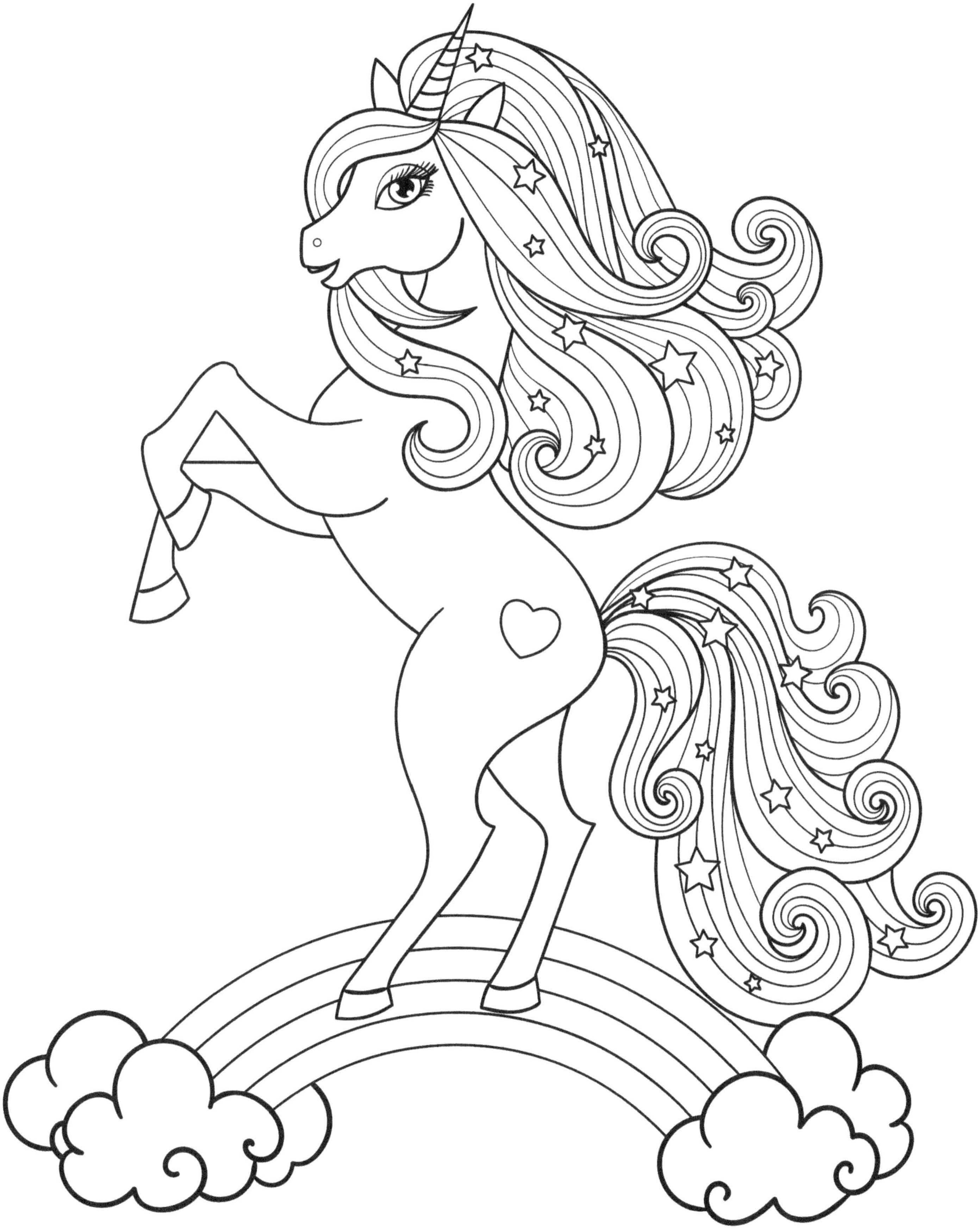

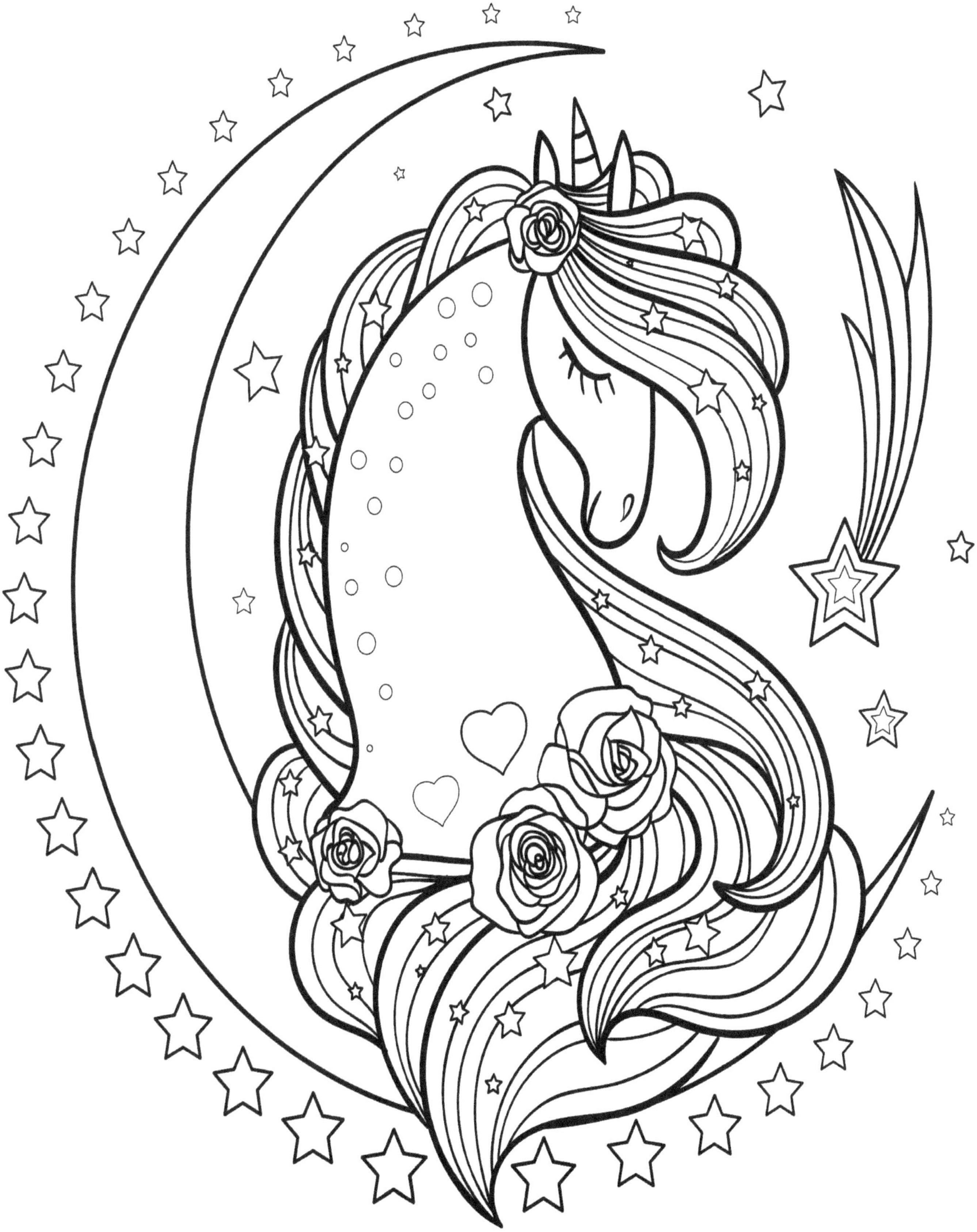

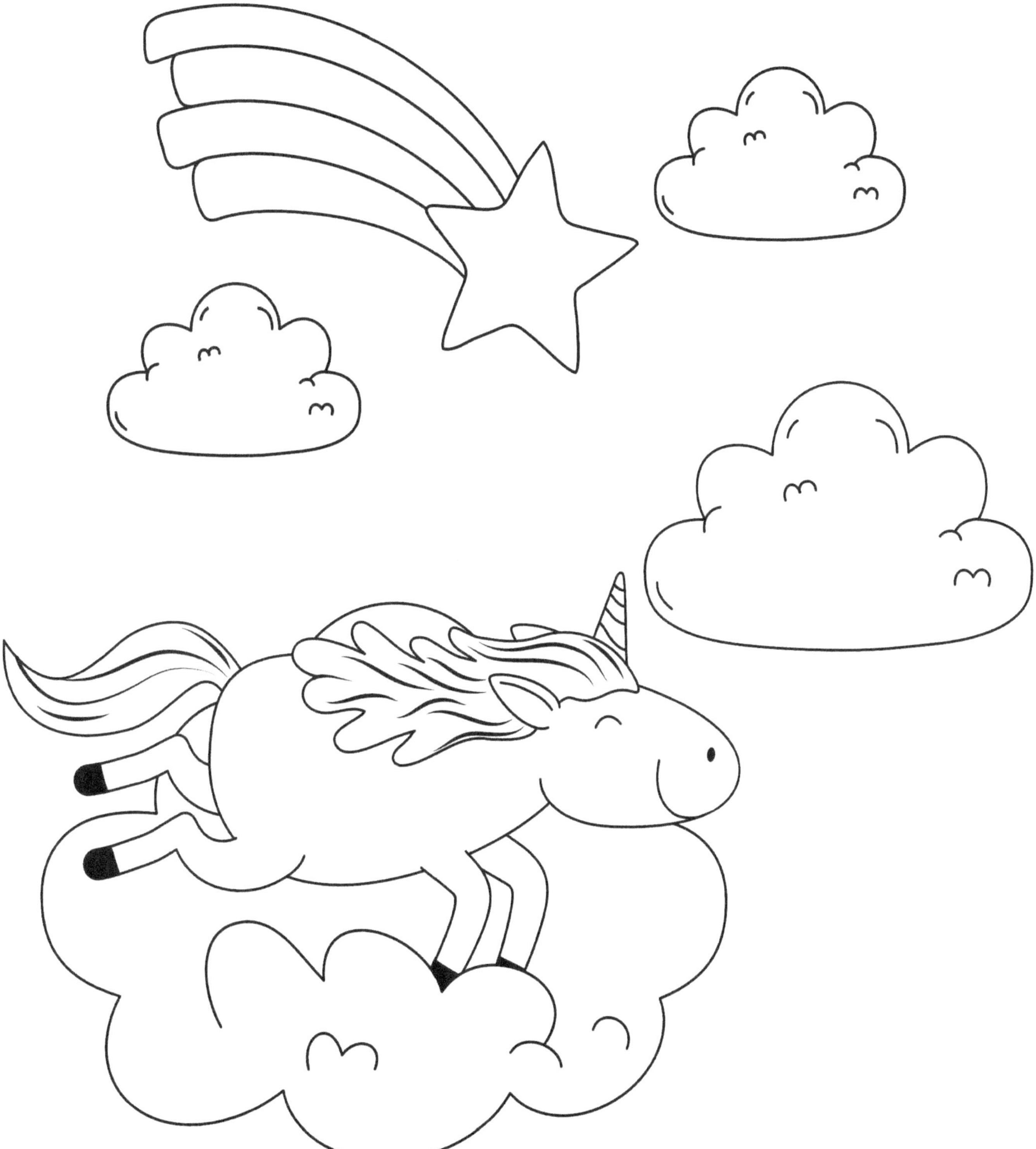

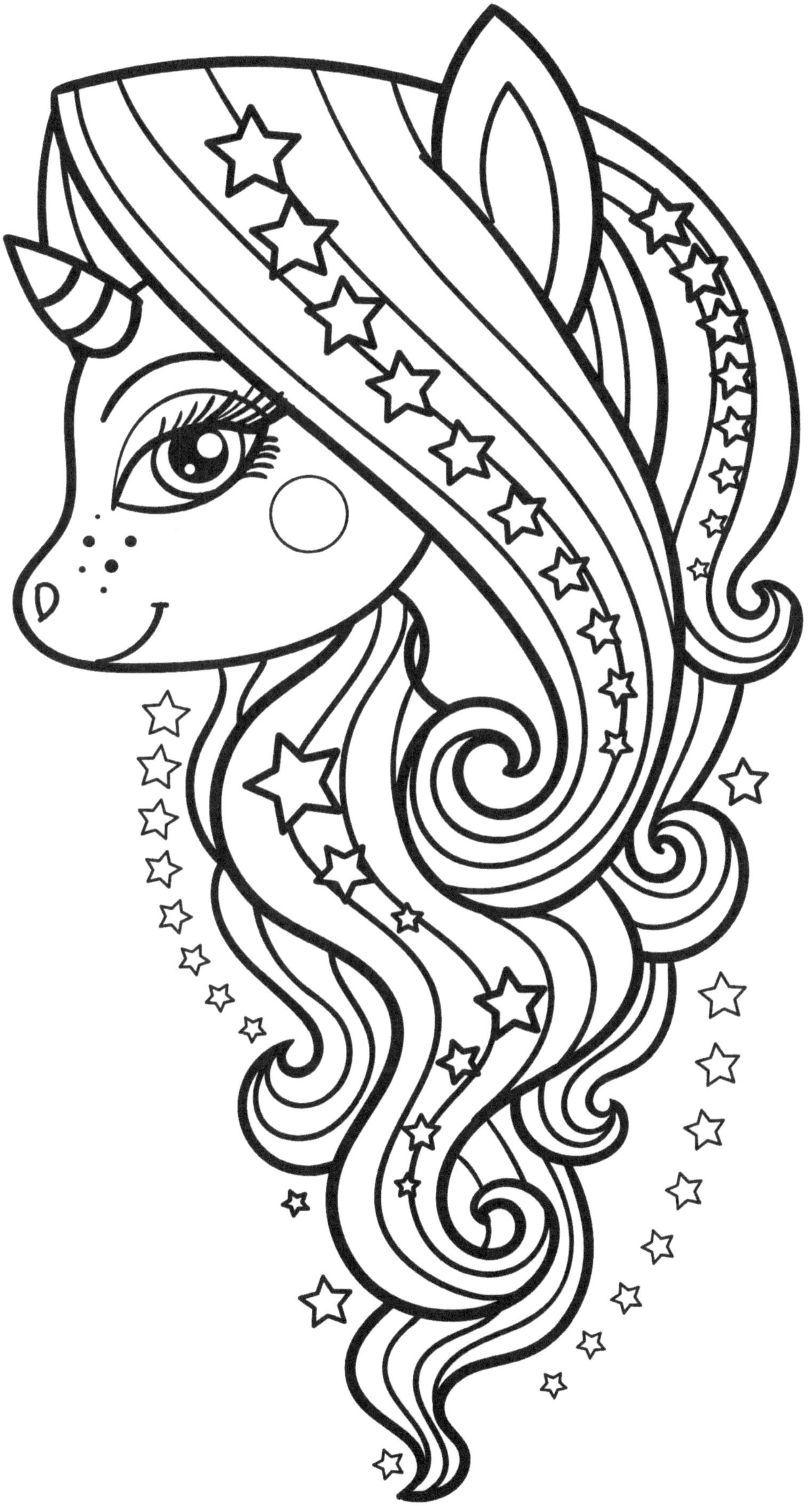

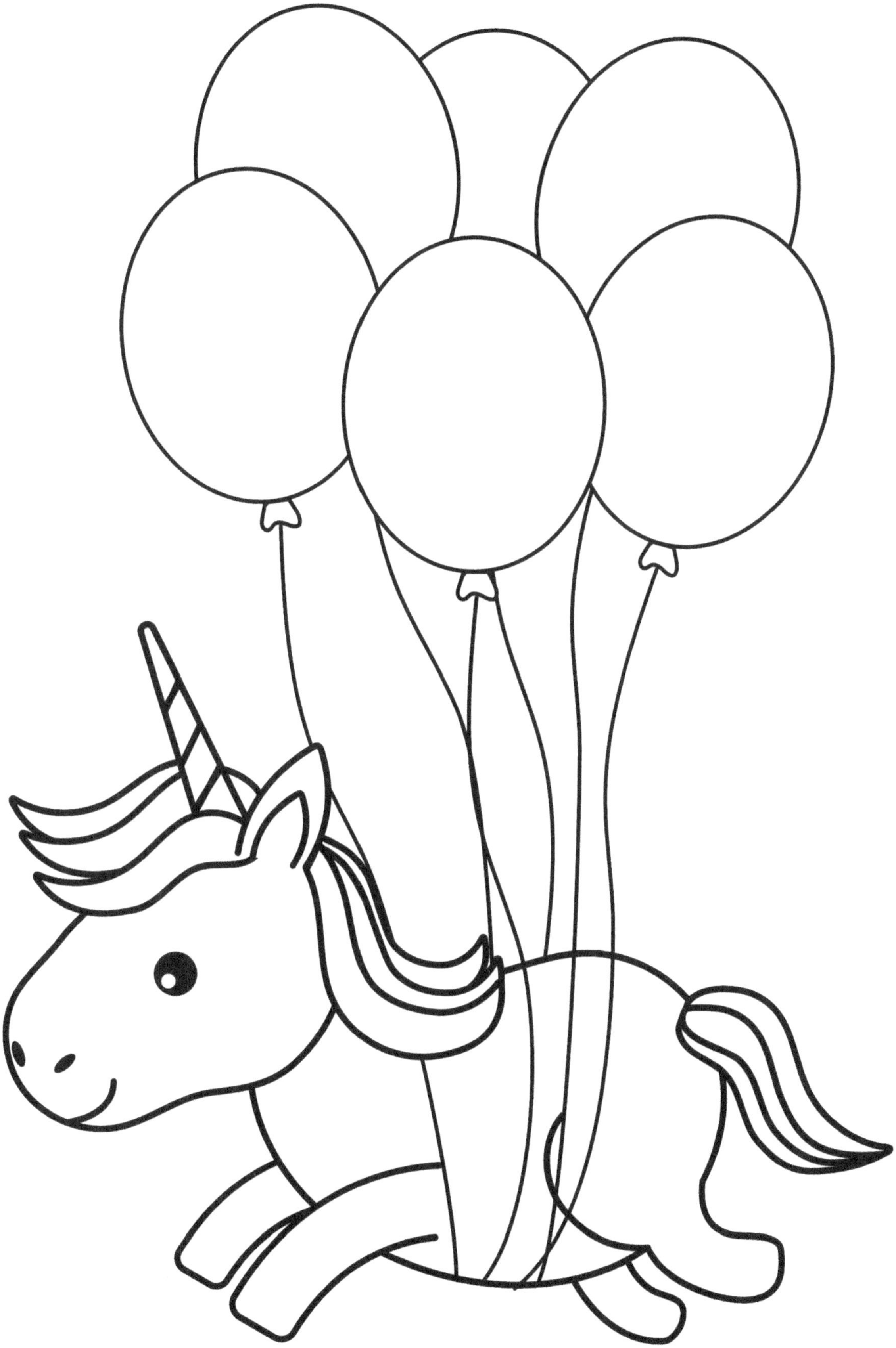

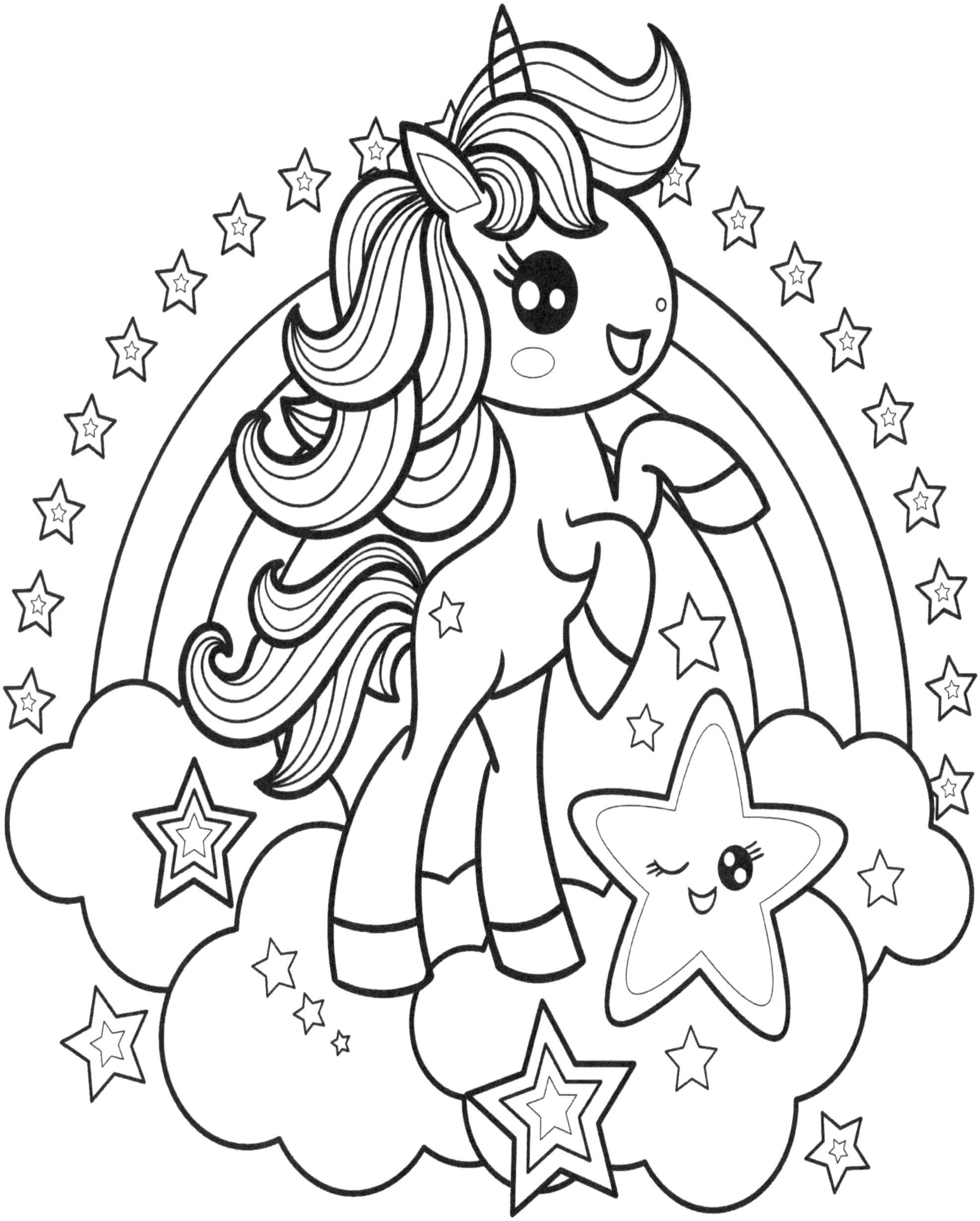

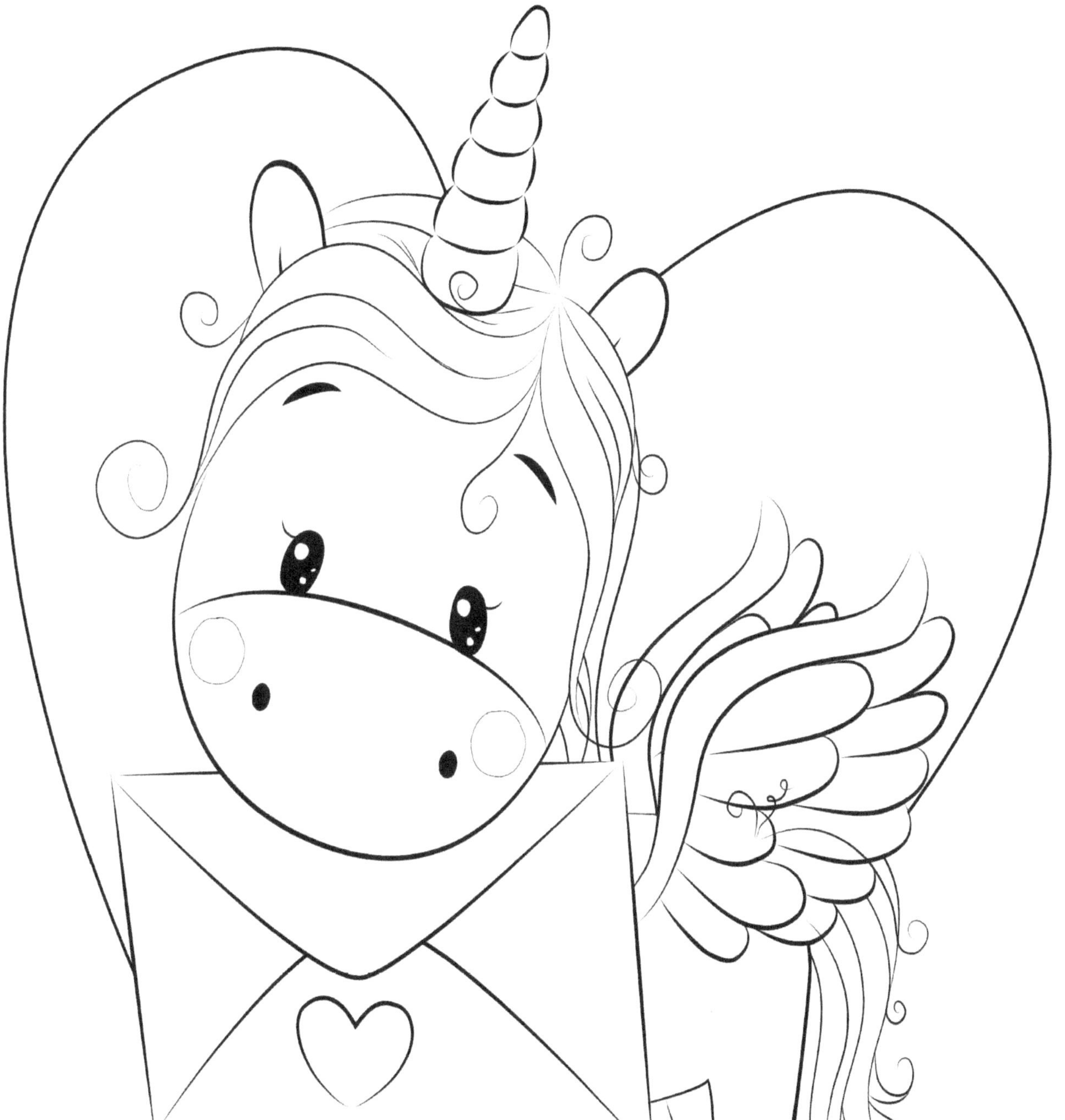

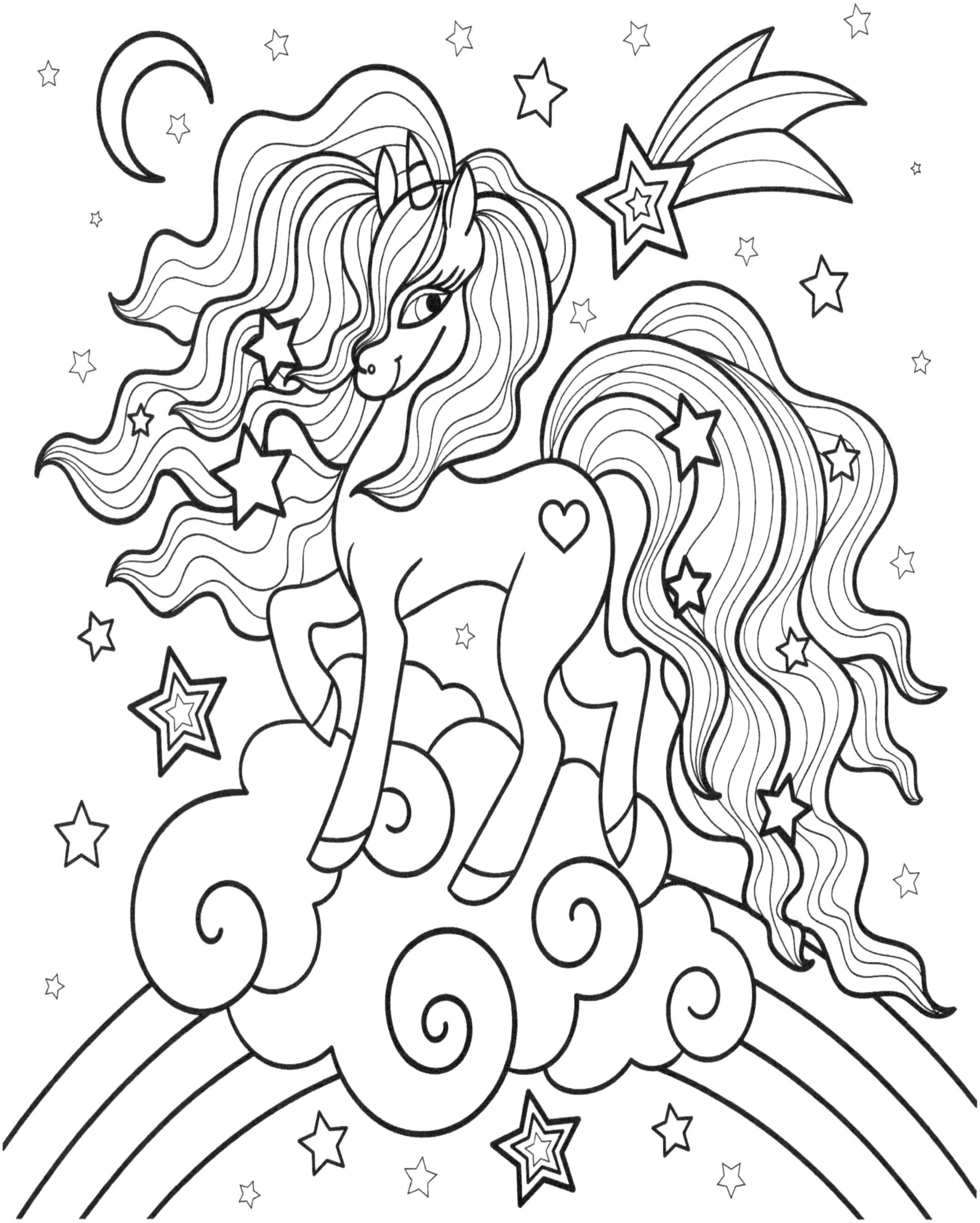

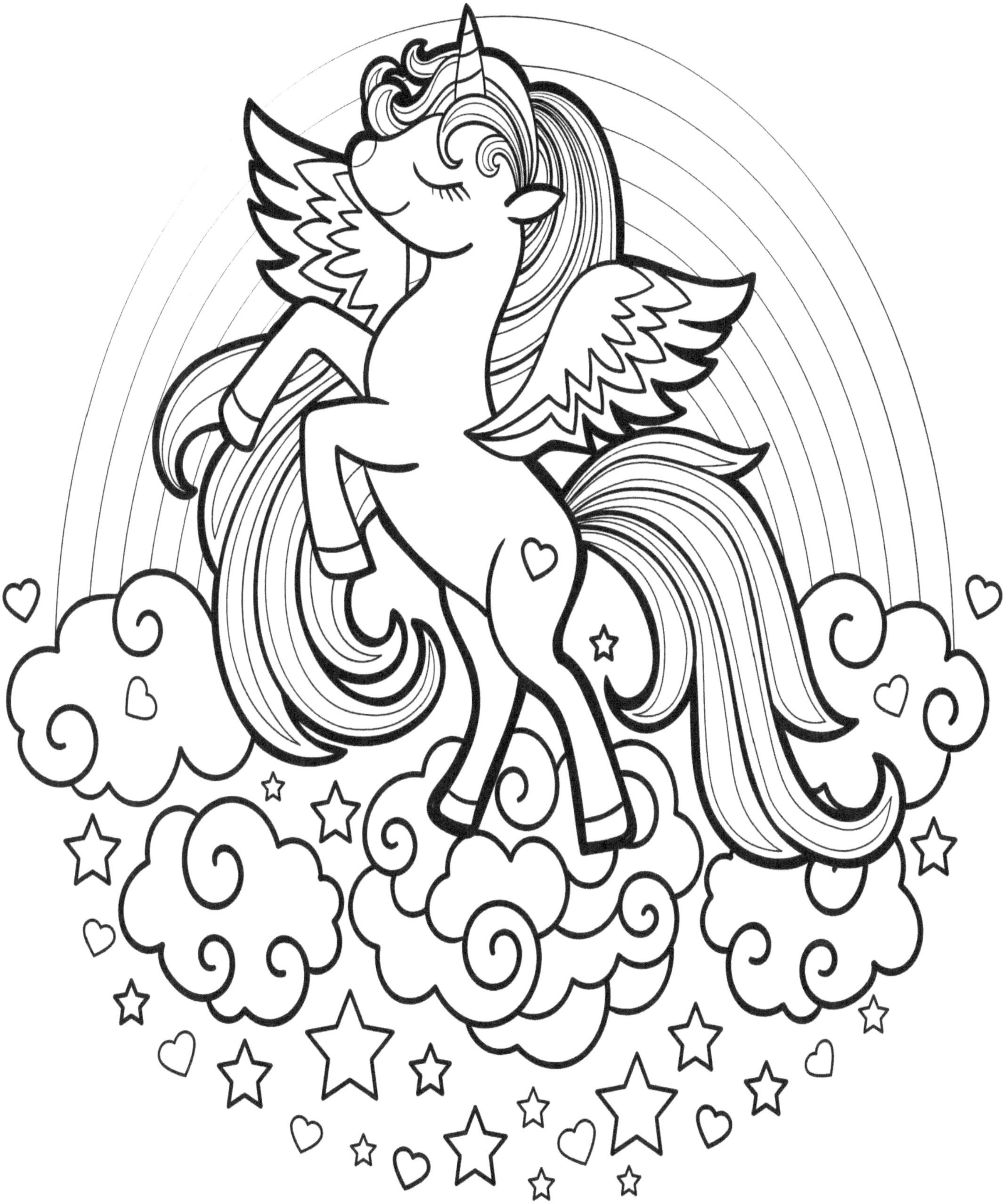

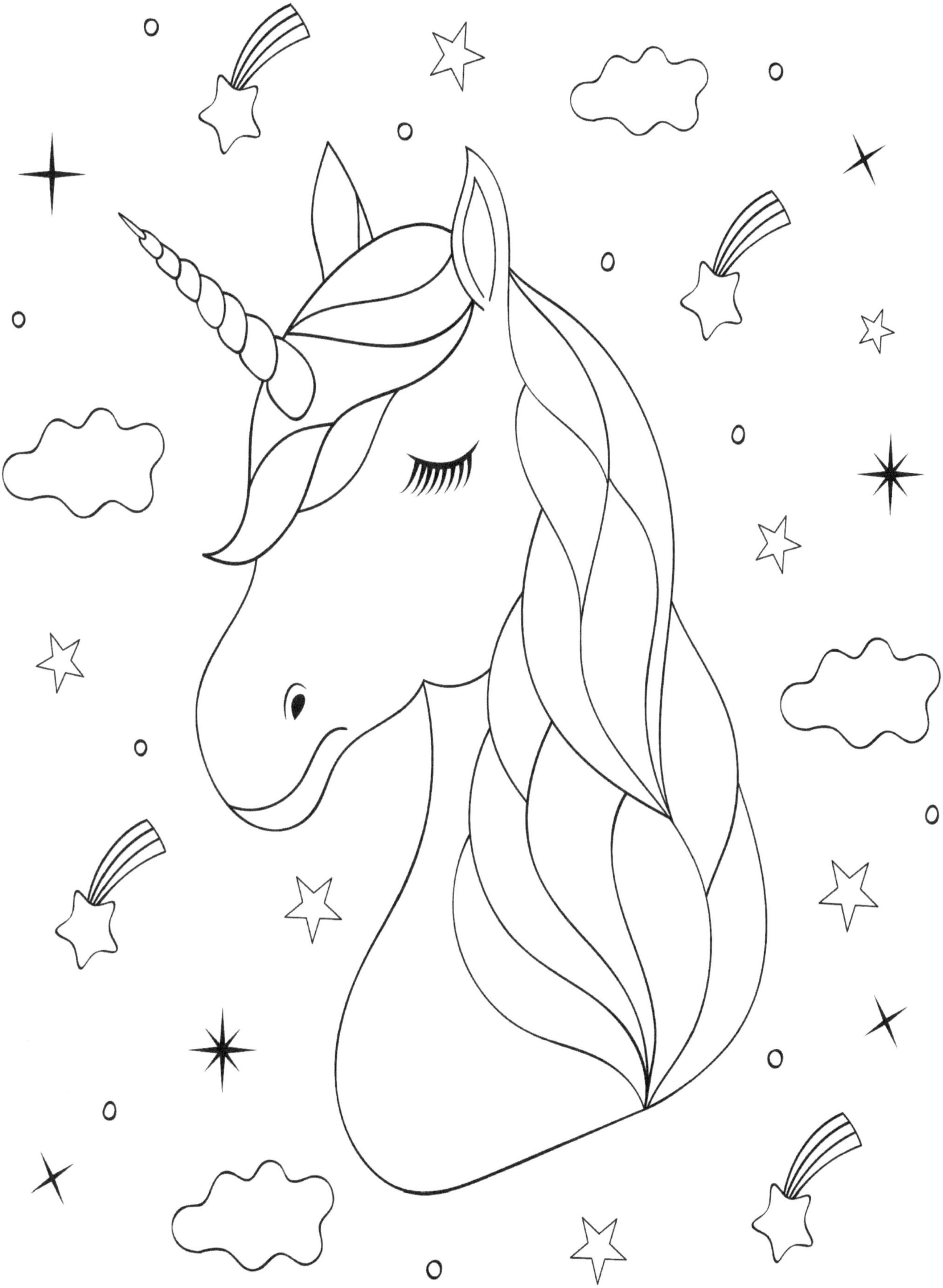

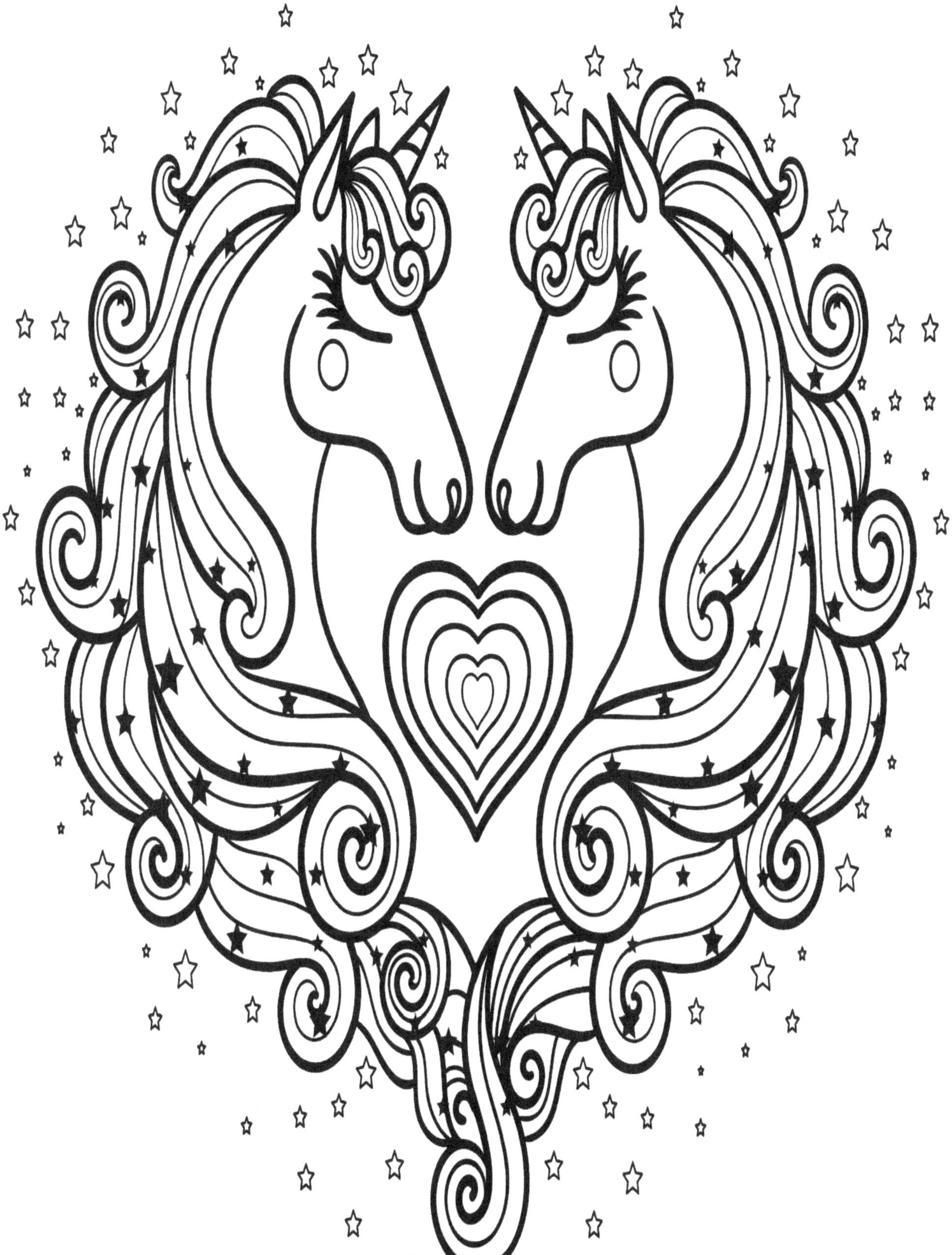

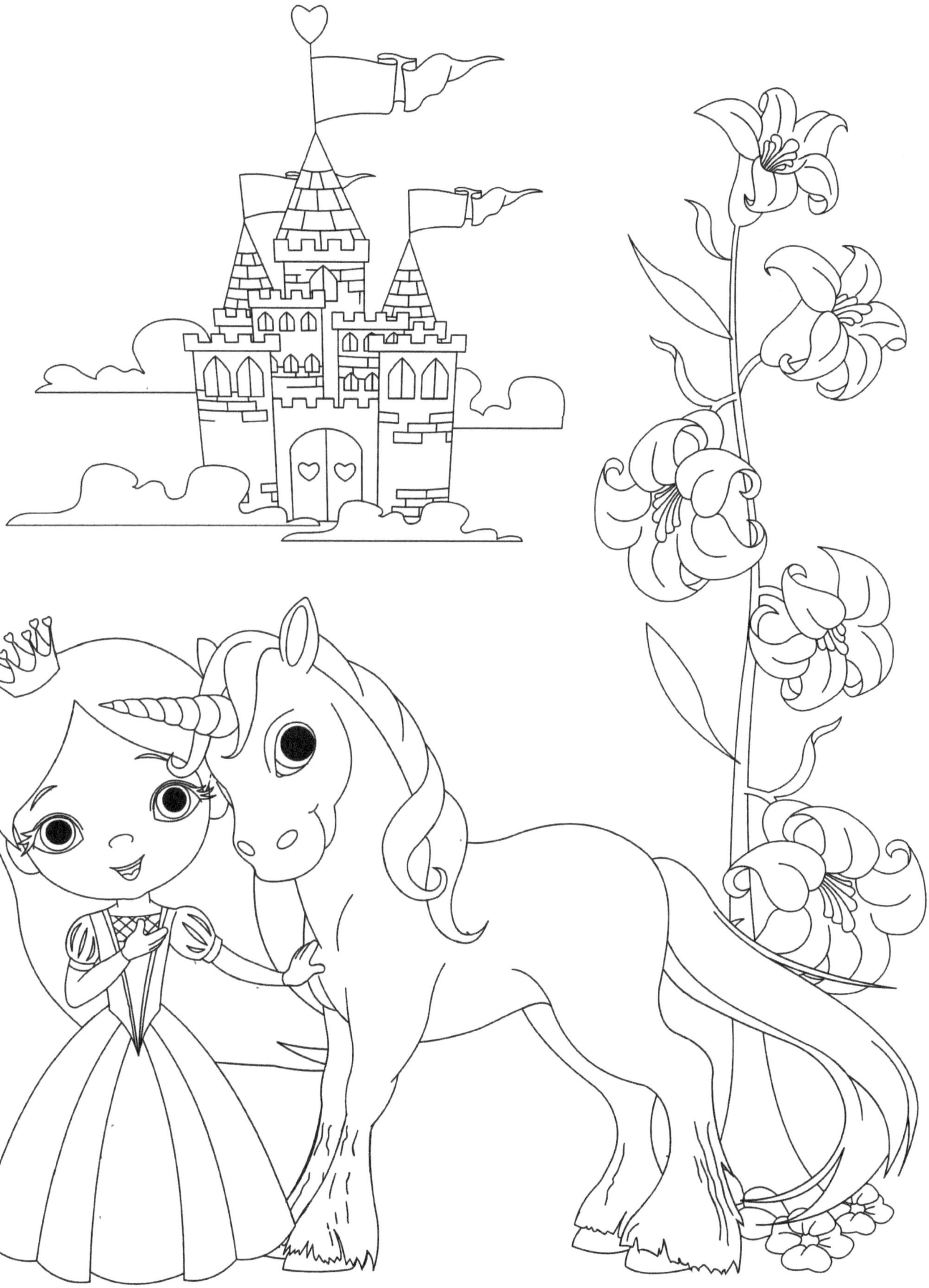

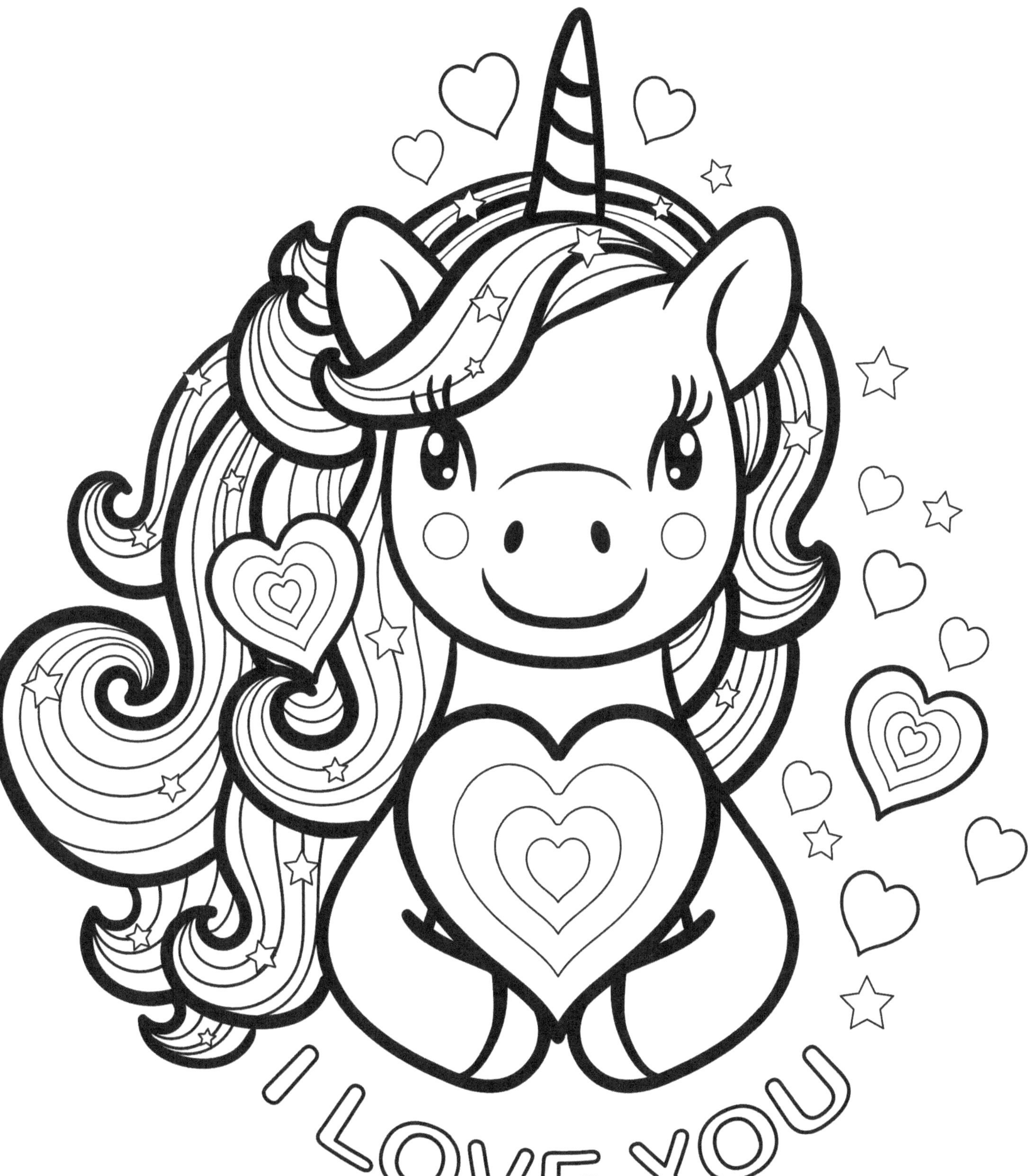
I LOVE YOU

www.ingramcontent.com/pod-product-compliance
Lightning Source LLC
Chambersburg PA
CBHW080551240526
45466CB00031B/3358
* 9 7 9 8 5 2 9 6 0 0 5 2 8 *